"This is such an important and needed book. Youn, *a tool for developing their independence successfully.* *Norene have published this invaluable resource as n* *are coming of age. I will make sure each and every o̶n̶e̶ o̶f̶ t̶h̶e̶m̶ a̶l̶o̶n̶g̶ w̶i̶t̶h̶ e̶v̶e̶r̶y̶ y̶o̶u̶n̶g̶* *person I love—is armed with* It's Your Mind: Own It!*"*

KATE BECKER – Director of the Seattle Office of Film + Music, co-founder of The Vera Project, and founder of The Old Fire House Teen Center

"I truly wish this book had existed when I was growing up. In clear, focused language, it illuminates the patterns that trap us in cycles of self-doubt and loathing, and gives us constructive ways out of the circle. Not just 'for kids,' it offers insight into many of the more common challenges we all face on a daily basis. Sievers and Gonsiewski have compiled a vital arsenal of tools for coping with the tricks our minds play on us in dealing with the world around us. If you're a teen, or have one, you owe it to yourself to read this book."

ADAM WALDMAN – Co-owner and creative director of the entertainment marketing creative agency The Refinery *www.therefinerycreative.com*

"What Nicole and Norene have drawn up here is the ultimate road map for a teenager. Navigating through the fear and loathing of being a teenager is something that I wouldn't wish on my worst enemy, and certainly something I would not ever wish to repeat. However, with this book, being a teenager could quite well become a pathway of excitement, achievement and knowledge. The authors have provided information that will help teenagers and young adults find their inner power, their sense of 'can do,' their strength and courage to seek out their own success. When I was growing up, being a rock star/poet/writer/ actor/anything left of center was simply not encouraged. It took a lot of tenacity and focus to ignore all the people who tried to tell me it 'can't be done' or that it's 'not a great choice.' If I had been given a copy of It's Your Mind: Own It! *my journey would have been a lot less painful and difficult. Most young people will benefit enormously from this book, and I am relieved that it now finally exists."*

BILLY MORRISON – Artist, actor, and guitarist for Billy Idol & Royal Machines *www.billymorrison.net*

"Adolescence is anything but easy! Reading this book, however, helped me to understand why I was thinking certain things and thinking in certain ways. It taught me that, when we recognize our motivations, when we anticipate our 'road blocks,' and when our 'navigation systems' are strong, we have a fighting chance. Even better, we might just thrive!"

GABRIEL HUNTER SENN – 19-year-old college student and intern with Stand For Courage

"Most every adult has, at some time, wondered what it would be like to go back in time to magically re-live their teenage years with the benefit of all they know now. The fantasy always involves embracing youth with less fear and a greater sense of what a person can achieve if they set their mind to it, but while most of us continue to dream Nicole and Norene have come up with the next best thing. In this owner's manual for the teenage mind lies all the simple and easy knowledge youth need to find their own perfect rhythm amidst the cacophony of modern life."

TOBY BARRAUD – Co-owner and executive producer of Eastern.tv and the wildly popular "Love & Hip Hop" *www.eastern.tv*

"Every teen should read It's Your Mind: Own It! In fact, I challenge all pediatricians to hand out this book during well-teen check-ups! The neuroscience-based tools shared in the book can help young people develop the skills they need to thrive and live authentic, fulfilling lives."

KATHY MASARIE, MD – Pediatrician and author of *Face to Face: Cultivating Kids' Social Lives in Today's Digital World*

"This book is a unique guide with an innovative program for teaching teens to deal with adolescent angst and anxiety. It's a perfect tool for teens (and for adults) to shift a difficult paradigm, and rarely are these issues tackled so straight forwardly and so youth friendly."

CHARLES R. CROSS – Rock historian, music critic, and *New York Times* bestselling author of *Heavier Than Heaven* and *Room Full of Mirrors*

"Trying to decide whether to buy or read this book? I'd give it to you as a gift if I could! Why? Because it helps you figure out when your mind is playing tricks on you and keeping you from having an awesome life. Give it a try!"

ERIC SIEVERS, MD – Children's cancer research doctor

"Own your mind. If you don't—someone else will. There is not much unclaimed real estate in this world. It is said that the greatest tool of an oppressor is the mind of the oppressed, so protect yourself. Bombarded by everything that makes this planet look and feel like a doomed place, it is hard to find motivation for the tedious things that adults claim to matter and harder still to find the courage to do your own thing. It's Your Mind: Own It! is a helpful, funny, informative, and practical book. My overall capacity is enhanced and my trust in the importance of my own contributions is magnified from reading it."

JACOB N.L. SENN – 17-year-old student of entrepreneurship, motivation, success, creativity and social justice; and Youth Advisory Board Member of Stand For Courage

It's Your Mind:
OWN IT!
A Manual for Every Teen

Nicole Jon Sievers, MSW, LCSW
Norene Gonsiewski, MSW, LCSW

With illustrations by Jesse Van Mouwerik

Innovations Press

Portland, Oregon

Editor and Production Coordinator
Ruth Matinko-Wald • matinkowald@msn.com

Illustrator
Jesse Van Mouwerik • jessevanmo@gmail.com

Cover and graphic design concept
Machele Brass • www.brassdesign.net

Interior graphic design and layout
Rachel Wald • rwald@u.rochester.edu

Innovations Press
2804 SW 28th Avenue
Portland, Oregon 97202
United States of America

Library of Congress Control Number: 2014950714
ISBN 978-0-692-25692-3
Printed in the United States of America

In loving memory of
Amelia Rose Gonsiewski Wenzel
(1982-2014)
Without her prodding and encouragement,
this body of work would not exist.

We also dedicate this book to our beloved sons
Alex, Gabe, Jake, Max, Nick, and Ben.

Watch your thoughts; they become words.
Watch your words; they become actions.
Watch your actions; they become habit.
Watch your habits; they become character.
Watch your character; it becomes your destiny.

– Lao Tzu

A Note to the Reader

Dear Reader,

We are so excited that this book is in your hands—even if some adult handed it to you and you're wondering, "Why bother reading another book for youth written by adults?" It's a good question! Please consider why we think this book is worth your time and was more than worth our time to write it.

As caring adults, we authors are personally driven to inspire you to live life as only you were meant to live it. We want you to have a life of your own design, to discover your own passion, to reach your own goals using your natural talents, to have great relationships, and to feel the joy and satisfaction of experiencing a good mood.

As counselors, however, we know certain thinking styles can prevent you from living a life full of energy, pleasure, creativity, innovation, resilience, and happiness. Automatic negative thoughts (ANTs) and negative self-talk can ruin self-esteem, inhibit your capacity to recognize and develop your unique gifts, and get in the way of connecting, and staying connected, with others. Limiting thought patterns also make it difficult to get motivated and to perform your best.

You are in the driver's seat! You have the choice whether you steer your life without unnecessary distractions and tap into your inner resources to create a life you love—or always feel like you're driving a bus full of chattering inner critics, rebels, naysayers, doubters, judgers, and slackers shouting out directions. The key to quieting the chattering is understanding your amazing brain. You absolutely can think your way to feeling curious about the day's potential when you awake, to setting and achieving goals, to forging good alliances, and to being happy. Our book can show you how. The time-tested tools and exercises we've included can help you to deal with your ANTs and empower you to steer confidently and comfortably as you navigate the road of life.

So, we don't just think bothering with this book is worth your time; we know it! We also know—whether you skim or read every word, do some or all of the "Rest Stop" exercises, commit to journaling about your experiences or just check out Jesse's fun illustrations—you will take from the pages something you need.

Go ahead and peek. It's your mind! Own it, expand it, understand it, and manifest the creative potential that is uniquely you.

Love,
Nicole and Norene

P.S. The first journey is your mind. The second journey is your co-creation of a world that works for everyone. We invite you to practice your newfound skills by committing to stand for courage for yourself, for your community, and for the world.

The proceeds from the sales of this book will be shared with Stand for Courage and with other nonprofit organizations that work to better our world.

Why? Because, for each of us to develop our unique gifts, we need both an inner and outer environment that is conducive to health in connection to ourselves as well as in relationship with others.

Contents

WELCOME TO YOUR "DRIVER'S MANUAL"

The road of life is the ultimate obstacle course. Sometimes the road will be smooth, and other times, bumpy. Although controlling life's twists and turns is impossible, how you respond to each crossroad or pothole can keep you moving forward on your desired course. Truly, you are in the driver's seat of your life. If you choose "automatic pilot," you will eventually run off the road, but if you drive using your inner resources, you'll navigate life with success and resiliency. Think of this book as your driver's manual of life!

One of the common roadblocks to feeling strong and composed is the belief that life happens to you and you have no choice in how you're left feeling. This is simply not accurate. Feelings are a direct result of how we interpret every single experience.

Do you ever wonder what controls your feelings? What *makes* you feel angry when someone calls you an idiot or *makes* you self-conscious when you walk into a crowded cafeteria? Well, it's the same process that *makes* you happy when someone you like sits by you at lunch, and the same process that *makes* you excited when you get your driver's license. All feelings are generated by the automatic **thoughts** that pop up when you experience life's gifts, and life's challenges. The way the process works is that your mind assesses and interprets a situation, and then, in reaction to your interpretation, your body sends out a shot of chemicals that cause you to feel a certain way.

In truth, **feelings** may seem to come from your heart or your guts, but they actually come from your head. Everyone walks around all day with ideas, stories, and impressions floating in and out of the mind. These "interpretations" trigger the chemicals and, ultimately, the feelings that flood you with positive and negative energy. If you become aware or "mindful" of what you think and take charge of the interpretation, you will be able to control your attitude and your reactions. In other words, it's your mind; own it… and take charge of your life. Doing so is the key to driving the road of life with confidence and ease—and to creating value for yourself and others along the way.

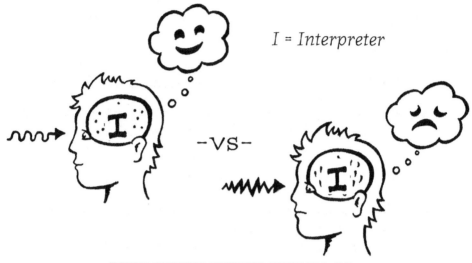

$I = Interpreter$

$-vs-$

EXPLORING UNDER THE HOOD

You're the driver of your life. Your mind is the engine. Let's take a look "under the hood" of this complex machine to understand how it works.

Many respectable theories exist explaining how brain function leads to what we experience as *feeling*. One simple and well-used theory dates back 2,000 years, to when a Greek philosopher by the name of Epictetus observed that feelings follow *after* thoughts. Over the years, brain science has evolved—and is evolving every day—to include new information on why we see things the way we do. No matter what new research brings in the future, however, the key to a positive outlook is to understand and manage the part of our brain that interprets our experiences.

Let's explore this idea further by considering the well-researched work of Aaron Beck and David Burns. For nearly half a century, their cognitive (power-of-thinking) theory has been consistently helpful in supporting sound mental health. According to Beck and Burns, **cognitive distortions** are inaccurate thoughts that reinforce negative thinking or emotions—telling us things that sound rational and accurate, but really only serve to keep us feeling bad about ourselves. Here's a rundown of the major ideas of cognitive theory:

1) Feelings and thoughts are not the same thing. In fact, feelings are *generated* by thoughts.

Thoughts are mental activities that result in ideas or arrangements of ideas. Although some thoughts are very fast and mostly signal safety or danger, all thoughts are full of interpretations that lead to stories, imagination, critical thinking, beliefs, and more. Research indicates that you have approximately 70,000 thoughts per day (UCLA Laboratory of Neuro Imaging, 2008). That's one thought every 1.2 seconds! Interestingly, some scientists believe that approximately 90% of what we think each day is exactly what we thought yesterday.

What is really cool is that thoughts then *generate* feelings. Yep, all feelings! Happiness, sense of safety, anger, self-hatred, prejudice, shyness, pride, depression, revenge, compassion, and love are all created by the thoughts that precede them. The way this works is that a part of the human brain is dedicated to making sense of things and to keeping us safe. We call this brain part "The Interpreter." When an event takes place, your "Interpreter" analyzes the details of your experience and, in response to the analysis or interpretation of the experience, sets off a series of chemical releases which lead to your feelings—and subsequent actions. The entire process usually happens within five seconds. In fact, more than 100,000 chemical reactions are going on in your body every second!

In essence, feelings are powerful chemical reactions. When a human's thought process interprets a situation as dangerous, for example, the brain forwards a message to adrenal glands to send out the hormone

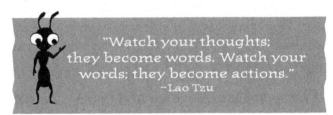

"Watch your thoughts; they become words. Watch your words; they become actions."
–Lao Tzu

adrenaline, which causes the human to react quickly and flee, freeze, or fight. If the sense of danger—or a negative interpretation—persists, then additional hormones of cortisol, testosterone, and noradrenaline are also released in high doses. A combination of these particular chemicals in various doses contributes to the creation of what we call *anger*. A slightly different chemical mix creates what we call *fear*. Similarly, when our mind interprets a situation as safe, our brain tells our glands to release the hormone serotonin, the chemical that helps to maintain a calm, happy mood.

2) All people have automatic negative thoughts, or ANTs, which are inaccurate.

All people have problematic interpretations or **automatic negative thoughts**. ANTs are so common, normal, and universal that they have been studied extensively and grouped into ten different categories, which we will discuss in the next chapter. They are called *negative* because they lead to unpleasant moods or feelings. In fact, ANTs are the cause of *all* our unpleasant feelings, including anxiety and depression. But ANTs are *inaccurate*. They are imbalanced and distorted views of life's highs and lows and lead to limiting interpretations.

Something else you may want to consider is that ANTs are *automatic*, which means they can happen without time to logically assess a particular situation, and they usually go unquestioned. Because we *think* something, we *assume* it is accurate. But that is not always the case.

Although we will examine more closely the origins of automatic negative thoughts later in this workbook, ANTs generally derive from:

- Beliefs of your family, friends, and community
- Influence of social media, movies, songs, and television
- Memories and experiences

Granted, your mind is your own, but the interpreting part of your brain reaches back into its "database" for analysis and pulls up what was recorded there. Sometimes your Interpreter is accurate in sizing up a situation—and sometimes not! Nonetheless, the Interpreter is always in charge of stimulating the feelings that will follow.

3) When you challenge an ANT and replace the problematic interpretation with a *realistic* interpretation, you change your mind and then your mood.

 This is very important information. *Because we cannot change or control events outside of us, the only control we have is how we interpret the events.* Challenging and replacing ANTs with realistic thoughts can reduce stress, brighten your mood, increase your self-confidence, and give you the motivation to reach your goals.

4) Actions can follow feelings, and those actions can have lasting consequences.

Behavior is driven by interpretations and the resulting feelings. When we feel upset, we can mistreat or withdraw from others, argue, make mistakes, give up on projects, or act in many other negative ways.

Here's an example of cognitive distortions in action. The example shows how things can unravel after an external, or outside, event.

Event Happens: A girl at school writes something unkind about Petra on her Facebook page.

Interpretation Follows: Petra's ANTs make her think, "Everyone is going to make fun of me! That girl is such a _____! My day is ruined! I can't go to school!"

Feelings (quickly) Follow: Petra feels embarrassed, shamed, sad, angry, fearful, self-conscious. (Remember, all these are different chemical reactions that result in what we call *feelings*.)

Behaviors (often) Follow: Petra withdraws from her peers, avoids group activities, treats someone else unkindly, or maybe acts with anger toward her sibling.

It's not that the situation wasn't unpleasant. No one enjoys rude comments, and such comments made publicly can be additionally painful. The problem lies in the magnitude of Petra's suffering. Petra *interpreted* the situation in a way that created negative feelings and then acted on those feelings as though they were all warranted. Yes, her feelings were *real*, but they were also by-products of how she viewed things. Instead, Petra could have acknowledged her ANTs for what they were—automatic *negative* thoughts—and chosen to replace them with a more realistic interpretation, and as a result responded to them differently. The bottom line is: *We can decide how we will view or interpret anything that happens. This, ultimately, gives us control over how we feel.*

The next example demonstrates cognitive distortion with an internal, or inside, event.

Event Happens: Washing your face in the morning and noticing a new outbreak of pimples.

Interpretation Follows: "Gross! I look terrible. My face is hideous. I can't go out looking like this…. I'm a freak. I always have the worst things happen."

Feelings (quickly) Follow: Shame, sadness, self-hatred, shyness.

Behaviors (often) Follow: Going to school (or finding an excuse not to go) and avoiding eye contact with that person you were flirting with yesterday, giving off the "leave me alone" vibe, and shielding your face when talking to him or her.

In both these scenarios, inaccurate interpretations filled with those pesky ANTs caused the problems. But they didn't need to cause problems! There are ways to control the ANTs, so they don't control you. There are powerful tools that can be used anywhere and anytime to change your mood, to dig you out of negative thinking, to help you feel better about yourself, others, and life in general.

YOUR TOOLKIT

The following chapters of this workbook explore common ANTs such as personalization and labeling. We will show you how to notice ANTs when they occur and how to examine whether or not the interpretations of the thoughts are valid. Once you notice (are mindful of) what you are thinking, you can gain control and decide how *you* want to view the situation by using a few simple tools we'll teach you. All the tools are easy to learn, but using them every day takes discipline. Eventually, these tools can help you be resilient. **Resiliency** is important to success in life. In its most simple definition, *resilience* is the ability to bounce back when you fall or are pushed down, having gained insight and strength from the situation.

We also have included exercises and journaling suggestions in each chapter, so the workbook has personal meaning for you and to reinforce the new tools you learn. You must put an honest effort into using the tools. No one can track, challenge, and replace your thoughts but YOU!

Life can be difficult and complicated, but, by paying attention to how you interpret experiences, you can have mastery over your life and drive with confidence! Take ownership of your mind, and you can improve your life!

REST STOP

REMEMBERING
Key words and phrases: Can you define them?

Thoughts_____

_____

Feelings _____

_____

Resiliency_____

_____

Automatic Negative Thoughts (ANTs) _____

_____

Cognitive Distortion_____

_____

_____

REFLECTING

Take time to ponder the following.

Do you believe you can really change how you feel? Are you open to learning how?

_____

_____

_____

_____

_____

What do you currently know about brain science and what it has to do with how you're feeling?

_____

_____

_____

_____

REINFORCING

Try these exercises to reinforce what you've learned.

1) When you catch yourself thinking a negative thought, try to pause and examine it for what it is, an ANT. Then, see if you can reframe the thought and rid yourself of the ANT.

2) Watch your favorite TV show and notice the negative thinking on the part of the characters. How do their negative thoughts affect the behaviors of the characters?

3) *Check out the following resource:* **Feeling Good: The New Mood Therapy** *by David D. Burns, MD.*

RECORDING AND RESOLVING
Journal writing is a great tool for dealing with ANTs.

Keep a journal of your automatic negative thoughts for one week. Just notice any negative thoughts you have. You'll learn how to "reframe" and exterminate them later in this manual.

_____

_____

_____

_____

_____

_____

_____

_____

_____

_____

_____

_____

_____

_____

_____

_____

_____

Remember:

| EVENTS → INTERPRETATIONS → FEELINGS → ACTIONS |

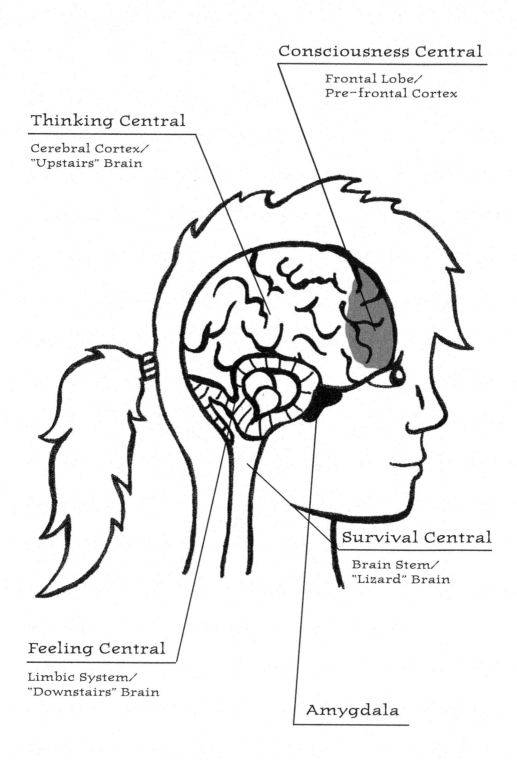

Thinking Central

Cerebral Cortex/
"Upstairs" Brain

Consciousness Central

Frontal Lobe/
Pre-frontal Cortex

Survival Central

Brain Stem/
"Lizard" Brain

Feeling Central

Limbic System/
"Downstairs" Brain

Amygdala

YOUR BRAIN: YOUR GREATEST ASSET

To understand how to use your mind to best navigate your life, you need to understand your greatest asset and how it works. Your brain is what makes you unique. It's central to who you are as a person. This incredibly complex organ controls your automatic bodily functions, your mood, your attitudes, your likes and dislikes, and even all your relationships.

In fact, the brain is actually more involved in your romantic relationships than your heart. When you are attracted to someone, you may believe your heart is responsible because it quickens or races when you see that person. But this only happens because your brain has millions of neurons, nerve cells that carry messages, in the pathways surrounding your heart.

The same is true of those sad times when you break up with someone or miss an important event. Your brain decides you should be sad and sends a different kind of message to those neurons around your heart, causing it to ache (Badenoch).

But managing your relationships is just one of the very interesting functions of your brain. Let's look at your brain's design and its other jobs.

Part 1

THE BRAIN IN GENERAL

The human brain evolved over a very long time, and, although it doesn't always work ideally, it is so amazing and successful that it has enabled a mammal not very physically powerful (us!) to dominate the planet. To keep a complicated subject simple, we will focus on the four major operating systems of the brain, what they do for you, and how they affect your quality of life, relationships, and moods.

SURVIVAL CENTRAL

The **reptilian (or lizard) brain**, which is shared by all animals from reptiles to humans, is Survival Central. In addition to keeping your heart beating and your lungs breathing, this part of the brain, physically "the brain stem," is concerned with one important question: "Is it safe, or is it dangerous?" It comes equipped with a giant "radar system," one that the military would envy. In fact, this part could be called your "lizard with radar." The bigger the radar, the better you will survive.

The main function of the reptilian brain is to scan the environment for clues as to whether or not it's safe. It "watches" facial expressions, body language, and the physical environment, and it uses sight, smell, taste, hearing, and touch. The reptilian brain doesn't take the time to check for accuracy; it reacts immediately.

For example, Brittany, who is on her high school track team, was on a daily run in her hometown, New York City. Out of the corner of her eye, she saw a striped bungee cord on the sidewalk. But her reptilian brain saw a cobra instead! Even though this doesn't make logical sense (because New York City is teeming with cobras, right?), Brittany's reptilian brain sent a message of danger, so she immediately leapt out of the way.

Before checking for accuracy, Brittany's brain protected her. The process happened instantly. Her heart began racing because Survival Central signaled the next part of her brain, Feeling Central, to let her know there was danger. She didn't have to think to get out of the way; her "lizard" saw danger and reacted—fast! But consider: The lizard was wrong. Almost simultaneously, Brittany realized what the lizard saw as a cobra was really a bungee cord, and, although her heart had begun racing, it quickly settled down, and she didn't think of it again.

FEELING CENTRAL

As noted above, Brittany's "lizard" brain signaled her Feeling Central part of the brain of potential danger. The Feeling Central part of the mammalian brain is the **limbic system** (also called the "downstairs" brain). It's in charge of releasing powerful chemicals that create feelings and sensations.

In essence, the limbic system is a "time traveler;" it doesn't relate to time or place. When it fires off and causes us to start feeling emotions, we don't know if this is caused by something that happened now, in the past, or even in the future.

How is this possible? This part of your brain stores your emotional memory. When something happens now that reminds you of the past, the neuron pathways that store memories related to the past event, whether pleasant or upsetting, will also fire off, intensifying the feelings you experience in that moment. Similarly, if a current event is tied to something you anticipate or expect in the future, you may experience emotions related to that anticipated event now (Stokes).

Like the reptilian brain, the limbic system isn't concerned with accuracy. When the lizard says, "Danger!" the limbic system doesn't ask, "Why?" or request proof. Instead, it quickly floods your blood stream with chemicals related to stress: cortisol and adrenaline. In response to commands from other parts of your brain, it can send feel-good chemicals such as oxytocin, dopamine, and serotonin.

Brittany's heart raced because the lizard told the limbic system to give her the right chemicals to flee or fight. As soon as she realized it wasn't a cobra, she took a deep breath. The limbic system stopped delivering cortisol and adrenaline, and the serotonin delivery system kicked in. She didn't need to *think* about any of this; her two brain systems most related to survival did it automatically for her.

THINKING CENTRAL

The **cerebral cortex**, or Thinking Central, is the part of your brain that's in charge of what you know of as "thinking." This includes the self-talk you take for granted, how you learn, and your ability to communicate. This part of the brain, also known as the "upstairs" brain, can send messages to the limbic system, not as fast as the reptile, but within five seconds. It's also wired with two kinds of memories: implicit memories and autobiographical memories.

Implicit memories, or unconscious memories, are memories of events that occurred before you had reason and perspective—and you have thousands of them. All the things that have happened to you since your birth are stored in your brain in the form of neuron pathways. But you can't remember most of them even if you try.

Implicit memories are also "time travelers," because these memories trigger the limbic system to fire off, causing us to experience emotions. But we don't realize these emotions are caused by an implicit memory. Instead, we think they are a reaction to what's happening right now, in this minute.

Your **autobiographical memories** are snippets and mental snapshots, and they do have time and context. An example of an autobiographical memory is remembering that your grandpa died when you were five, causing you to feel sad now when you recall the event. You know you are currently feeling sad about a past loss.

On the other hand, if you were one year old and suddenly lost your grandpa who took care of you every day, you won't really remember it. But you may now have a vague sense that you could lose someone upon whom you depend. Now, if an event occurs in which you think someone is leaving you, your implicit memories of grandpa's death fire off, but you don't realize this. Instead, you think what you're feeling is all about what's happening now. That makes you feel worse than the current situation calls for, and unconsciously you might avoid getting close to people.

CONSCIOUSNESS CENTRAL

The last part of the brain we want you to understand is the **frontal lobe**, Consciousness Central. Among other things, the frontal lobe (home of the prefrontal cortex) is responsible for self-awareness. It's the only part of the brain that can witness what you are doing, answer the question of why you are doing it, and do a check-in as to whether what you are thinking and feeling is accurate, logical, reasonable, and productive. This part of the brain is the most capable of understanding the rest of the brain.

> **INTERESTING FACT**
>
> Dogs also have a developed frontal lobe. This is what enables them to read humans well and come over to lick your face when you're sad.

The frontal lobe is where you experience compassion (for yourself and others), sympathy, empathy, concern, and the desire to comfort others. It's also the part that reads other people's emotions and understands that you and other people are experiencing events differently. The other parts of your brain don't really get that. The other parts of your brain automatically assume that others think and feel as you do.

PUTTING IT ALL TOGETHER

So what part of the brain is in charge of your friendships and other relationships? It seems like it might be the frontal lobe. Given that the frontal lobe helps you to read others accurately and to be concerned about them, that must mean we relate to friends, parents, partners, and teachers from Consciousness Central, right? Let's find out.

When you are relating to another human being and having a great time, the four parts of your brain are in balance and in good communication. The lizard doesn't see any danger, so it's lying on a rock in the sun; Feeling Central is sending out chemicals of peace and harmony; and you are having good thoughts filled with contentment. Your Consciousness Central knows that other people have a right to be who they are, and it's all good. This is called **brain integration.** All parts are communicating with one another well, and things are fine—until something happens that signals danger.

The perception of danger can be as simple as you seeing a look on your friend's face that tells you she is judging you. You see "that look," and guess what? Your "lizard with radar" says, "Danger! Your friend is frowning! Yikes, that is definitely dangerous!" Very quickly, your brain integration ceases. The two most basic parts of your brain, reptilian and limbic, take over. This means that most of the blood flow in your brain goes to those two parts, and little blood flows into your higher functioning parts of thinking and consciousness. What's important to note is that the less blood in the area, the less ability there is to utilize that area of the brain!

When your lizard and limbic system take over, you start time traveling, searching for all the memories about disapproval you have stored, implicitly or autobiographically. And because, of course, you were a normal little kid, you did lots of things that resulted in parental disapproval. Now all of those memories and the emotions associated with them fire off in your brain, and your brain tells your glands to pump out stress chemicals. Once those chemicals are in your bloodstream, which takes all of five seconds (Burns), then you go into "survival mode."

Once in survival mode, you'll begin to react from one of the human defense systems: flight, fight, freeze, hide, or submit. You might leave the situation in a hurry (flight), become defensive (fight), or grow quiet and go into your shell (hide). In the meantime, your friend reads your response to her perceived disapproval and

makes up her own story about what's happening! Good grief, this can go on all day, and it isn't just the frontal lobe that's involved in your interpretations. All four parts of the brain play a role.

All this over a glance your brain interpreted as dangerous! You may not even have read the look correctly. Your friend may have just realized she left her homework at home.

YOU CAN TAKE CONTROL!

So what is the way out when a negative event (or an event we believe is negative) occurs? How can we use our brains so they work for us rather than against us?

First, when we are upset, we need to get our brain working with all four parts. An animal regains brain integration by *noticing* the danger has passed and *taking a deep breath*. We do this, too. That's what a sigh does for us; we can take a deep breath and calm down.

The process of calming down is different for males and females, because there are biological differences. The stress hormones cortisol and adrenaline both bond molecularly with testosterone in the blood stream. Because males have more testosterone than females, this bonding means it takes boys about four times longer to calm down; it takes more time to break the bonds and clear out the stress hormones.

In the wild, these chemicals helped males to fight or take down an animal, so it made sense the chemicals would act longer in their systems. So when a male friend takes longer to calm down after becoming upset, it's important you don't take it personally. He isn't necessarily trying to punish you. In fact, he may be trying to protect you from his fight reflex by taking the time required to calm down.

A RECAP OF THE BRAIN

When all is going well, the four parts of your brain work together in harmony. As soon as the lizard sees danger—and the lizard often jumps to that conclusion unnecessarily—the parts of the brain stop working together; only Survival Central and Feeling Central function. Some researchers call this "flipping your lid" (Siegel). This means you don't have a good grasp of the situation. You have a limited ability to understand what's happening. You may experience a flood of memories, many of which are unconscious, and your feelings may take over.

All the parts of the brain are necessary for optimal functioning, but the lizard is always in charge. The parts of the brain involved in higher reasoning only get to chime in when the lizard thinks it's safe enough to take the time to listen.

When the lizard is in control and triggers a "danger" message, you need to do something to calm yourself to accurately assess the situation. Stop and breathe deeply. Take a walk around the block. Write down your thoughts and feelings. Or ask someone for his/her take on things. Any of these actions will signal to the "lizard" that you're really safe, and then your limbic system will send out a better cocktail of chemicals, one that makes you feel relaxed and secure.

Part 2

HOW YOUR BRAIN CHANGES IN ADOLESCENCE

As you go through adolescence, it becomes fairly obvious your body is changing. You can see the differences. What's less apparent is that your brain is going through significant changes as well. It's not just your body that's maturing; so is your mind.

Important changes in the brain's structure and functioning take place later in development than previously believed. Although the parts of our brains involved in cognitive processes (obtaining and storing information) fully mature by mid-adolescence, systems related to how we self-regulate, or handle our emotions, don't reach full maturity until late adolescence or even early adulthood. In a nutshell, humans mature intellectually before they mature emotionally or socially. This means you can be incredibly smart but still not have a full understanding of how to handle your feelings.

FOUR STRUCTURAL CHANGES IN YOUR BRAIN

If you could look into your brain during adolescence, you would be able to see some of the changes taking place. They are actual physical changes to the parts of your brain. As your body is changing shape on the outside, your brain is changing shape on the inside.

Let's take a peek at four major changes:

1. Out with the Old

Neurons are the cells that process and transmit information in your brain. From around the age of 9 until 15, your brain is deciding which connections between these neurons are important. Those that are damaged, not working well, or rarely used are eliminated. In fact, half of your neurons won't survive into adulthood! The principle "Use it or lose it" aptly applies to adolescent brain growth.

This process is called **synaptic pruning**. It may sound like a bad thing, but it's not. Skills you want to hold on to can be practiced and honed. For example, during adolescence and young adulthood, individuals hone musical, mathematical, athletic, and other skills if they practice often enough. Also, through regular face-to-face and shoulder-to-shoulder engagement, they can develop healthy, hearty social/emotional intelligence.

In essence, the synaptic process is believed to represent learning. By removing unnecessary neurons, your brain can operate more efficiently, giving you the ability to understand more complex ideas, to focus on a single problem or skill for longer, and to improve cognitive abilities and logical reasoning.

INTERESTING FACT

"Neurons that fire together wire together."
- Based on the work of Donald Hebb

2. In with the New

Don't worry that something is being taken away, because at the same time, your brain is getting something new: myelin. This white, fatty layer, also known as white matter, covers and protects your nerve fibers, allowing them to transmit data faster and more efficiently. This brain change is associated with the development of higher-order cognitive functions such as planning ahead, considering risks and rewards, and making complicated decisions.

The process is called **myelination** and continues longer than synaptic pruning, lasting until early adulthood. That means your brain's ability to make decisions that might impact your future is still maturing, even after your teen years.

3. A Focus on Pleasure

Particularly around the time puberty occurs, there are major changes that happen in the way the limbic system (Feeling Central) communicates with the frontal lobe (Consciousness Central). One significant change is that you are more sensitive to dopamine, a brain chemical associated with feelings of pleasure. In fact, you're more sensitive to dopamine during puberty than at any other time in your development. That means you're more motivated to seek situations that trigger the release of dopamine, even if they aren't good for you. We'll go more in depth about how this can affect your behavior in the next section of this chapter.

4. Stronger Connections

Another of the changes happening between your limbic system and your frontal lobe is that the connections between them are growing stronger. This helps to improve communication between the system that processes your emotions and the system that's important for self-control. In effect, your brain is getting an "upgrade" with newer, better "wiring" connecting the two regions.

Part 3

CHANGES IN HOW YOUR BRAIN WORKS

Now that you know what physical changes happen, you may be wondering how it affects how your brain works. Technology allows us to measure brain activity by looking at changes in blood flow. Let's take a look at what scans have revealed about the brain as well as about the functional changes that occur during adolescence.

THE PLEASURE CIRCUIT

When an experience causes dopamine to be released in your brain, it sets in motion several things:

- You will like the experience; it will be felt as pleasurable.

- Your brain will remember and associate everything about the experience with positive feelings: external sensory cues (sights, smells, tastes, sounds, and tactile sensations) and internal cues (thoughts and feelings). This process helps you to learn what you need to do to get that positive feeling again.

• You then assign a value for the pleasurable experience—ranging from a little pleasurable to very pleasurable—so you have a gauge to use when choosing between experiences. (Would you rather stay at home or go to an amusement park?)

This process is called the Pleasure Circuit, and it's interwoven with brain centers involved in decision making, planning, emotion, and memory storage.

The Pleasure Circuit helps us to decide what effort we are willing to make and what risk we are willing to take to get a similar experience again. The Pleasure Circuit is important for our survival as individuals and a species; it's designed to reward basic behaviors such as eating, drinking, and mating that are necessary for us to live and procreate. For example, early humans had to decide if they would risk hunting prey in order to have the pleasure of eating a meal. Today, most of these behaviors don't require much risk. You can simply open the fridge or head to a restaurant, but the same systems apply.

Over hundreds of millions of years, the biochemistry of pleasure has endured because it is so effective at driving behavior. Pleasure animates our lives. We associate pleasure with memory, emotions, social meaning, sights, and sounds. It's the Pleasure Circuit that's also behind our desire to engage in other healthy behaviors such as exercise, meditation, prayer, seeking social approval, and performing service to others.

What's interesting is that even witnessing something positive happening to someone else can cause the brain pleasure. The brain doesn't know the difference between what's real and what we believe is real. Special neurons, called **mirror neurons**, fire both when you act and when you observe someone else taking that action. This is why movies can make such a big impact on us; to our brains, it's as though those actions have happened to us. When you see characters living "happily ever after," your brain experiences their pleasure, too.

IMPORTANT FACTS ABOUT YOUR BRAIN

The more you know about the changes going on in your brain, the better prepared you will be to recognize poor decision making. Here are a few more quick facts to help you better understand what's going on inside your head as well as some tips to cope with the changes:

1. Approximately 30% of the cells in your cerebral cortex are pruned and replaced during adolescence. This can cause you to be confused or more forgetful. Ways around this? Create systems to help such as reminder notes and checklists.

2. The brain isn't fully developed until approximately age 24 in males and 22 in females. Don't be afraid to seek the guidance of a trusted adult for major decisions.

3. A diversity of experiences will help to better "wire" your brain. Try many different activities and sports to optimize your development.

4. Alcohol and drugs have a profound negative effect on the brain during adolescence. Ignore that dopamine rush and make a choice that's better for you in the long run.

5. Teens are especially prone to experience situations with their **amygdala** (the emotional center of the brain), which can cause you to be overly sensitive or personalize things. Take a deep breath and notice if you are thinking something negative. Perhaps your thought is not accurate. Try to relax before reacting.

6. Adolescent males experience an increase in testosterone, which can cause negative and aggressive thoughts. Adolescent females experience an increase in estrogen, which can cause moodiness.

VICE STIMULI

Unfortunately, sometimes the Pleasure Circuit works against us. After all, not every pleasurable experience is good for us. It may be more pleasurable to eat ice cream than broccoli, but broccoli is the healthier option.

Negative things that activate the brain's pleasure circuitry are called **vice stimuli**. Sugar, salt, drugs, unprotected sex, and risky behaviors such as driving over the speed limit are all examples. As far as dopamine is concerned, both healthy and unhealthy behaviors are the same. Whether you're volunteering at a local animal shelter or drag racing down a deserted road, it's the Pleasure Circuit that drives your behavior. Regardless of the path you take to get there, the feeling of pleasure remains your compass.

Unfortunately, the Pleasure Circuit leads many adolescents (and many adults!) to make decisions that can cause them long-term harm for short-term pleasure. For example, if, for every meal, we listened to the Pleasure Circuit and opted for ice cream instead of broccoli, our health would be negatively affected, which wouldn't be very pleasurable! Taking drugs is a good example as well. Many illegal substances cause us to feel good while we're using them, but we run the risk of serious consequences to our health, including death.

So it's important we engage other areas of our brains when making decisions, weighing the possible consequences of our actions versus how those actions make us feel in the moment. Something may feel good now, but what about an hour from now, a day from now, or even several years down the road?

During adolescence, the Pleasure Circuit is at its most sensitive. Because of the structural changes happening in the brain, adolescents experience higher levels of dopamine activity. More than at any other time in your life, you are motivated by seeking pleasurable experiences. Some studies have shown that this is particularly true when adolescents are in groups, which means you're more inclined to choose risky behavior when you're with friends.

So, why is the adolescent body so "keyed up" for seeking pleasure? The same reason other mammals experience this during puberty: to encourage mating. Sexual activity is motivated by pleasure, so it makes sense to increase our sensitivity to pleasure after puberty, further encouraging us to reproduce while at peak fertility. In nature, this may require taking risky behaviors such as leaving the nest or the pack to find a mate. What does this mean in terms of humans, for you?

OVERCOMING THE LIZARD IN CHARGE: DEVELOPING SELF-REGULATION

What makes the human brain different from other species is that our **prefrontal cortex**, the region that controls judgment and planning located in our frontal lobe, is bigger. The prefrontal cortex enables us to override the messages sent by our emotions (limbic system) to avoid choices that may be pleasurable in the short-term but aren't very good for us in the long-term. This process is called **self-control or self-regulation**.

Of course, this process isn't always easy. As we explained earlier, when humans experience an increase in heart rate, even a small one such as when we get angry or feel threatened, our primitive lizard brain takes over and reacts on instinct, triggering the flight, fight, or freeze response. Because it's an automatic response, we don't think before we act.

Granted, in the wild, this helped us to survive. You don't want to waste precious seconds weighing your options when threatened by a predator. You just want to take action. Either get out of there or fight back! But in modern society, our lizard brain often works against us. Thinking calmly and rationally about a situation usually results in a better response!

Because the ability for self-regulating is still maturing in the adolescent brain, teens have less "cross talk" between the parts of the brain that regulate emotional arousal (Survival Central and Feeling Central) and those that make rational decisions (Thinking Central and Consciousness Central). Without being kept in line by the brain regions that help to control impulses, plan ahead, and weigh risk versus reward, strong feelings can easily take over. That can mean a heart rate increase, and . . . you might as well hand control over to that reptilian brain on a silver plate.

Between the ages of 15 and 17, in fact, you're particularly susceptible to giving into the lizard brain. It's at that point in your life when your Pleasure Circuit is at its highest sensitivity, but the systems for self-regulation are still immature. It's like the brain's accelerator is pressed to the floor, but you don't yet have a good braking system installed!

This is likely why many risky and reckless behaviors peak at the age of 17:

- Committing crimes
- First experimentation with alcohol and marijuana
- Car crashes
- Accidental drowning
- Attempted suicide
- Unprotected sex

Ultimately, understanding your brain can help you recognize when your actions are being driven by your Pleasure Circuit or your reptilian brain. You can work to gain control over the decisions you make. The next chapter will tell you how.

REST STOP

REMEMBERING
Key words and phrases: Can you define them?

Reptilian/Lizard Brain _____

_____

Implicit Memories _____

_____

Autobiographical Memories _____

_____

_____

Self-Regulation _____

_____

Vice-Stimuli _____

_____

Brain Integration _____

_____

REFLECTING
Take time to ponder the following.

How old are you? Where are you on the continuum of brain development and the continuum of learning to self-regulate? What does this mean for how you make decisions, respond to stressful situations, or tackle challenging projects?

_____

_____

_____

_____

_____

Is there a particular person who routinely triggers you to be angry or upset? If so, consider the parts of the brain you typically use in responding to that person. Do you just "flip your lid" with him/her or do you engage your Thinking and Consciousness centers and consider his/her feelings as well as your own?

_____

_____

_____

_____

Is there a particular situation that routinely triggers you to be depressed, embarrassed, or frustrated? If so, reflect upon whether or not implicit or autobiographical memories might be involved with the trigger.

_____

_____

_____

_____

_____

REINFORCING

Try these exercises to reinforce what you've learned.

1) Name the four main parts of the brain. Explain how each of them may respond to an event that could be dangerous.

_____

_____

_____

_____

_____

_____

_____

2) Check out the following resource: **Brainstorm: The Power and Purpose of the Teenage Brain** *by Daniel J. Siegel, MD.*

RECORDING AND RESOLVING

Journal writing is a great tool for learning how to control your thoughts and feelings.

For a week, keep a journal of difficult and challenging situations. Identify each situation, name the feeling(s) generated, and note how you reacted to the particular situation. Then try to determine which "center" of the brain you used to respond.

_____

_____

_____

_____

_____

_____

_____

_____

_____

_____

_____

_____

_____

_____

_____

_____

_____

_____

_____

_____

_____

_____

_____

Remember:

EVENTS → INTERPRETATIONS → FEELINGS → ACTIONS

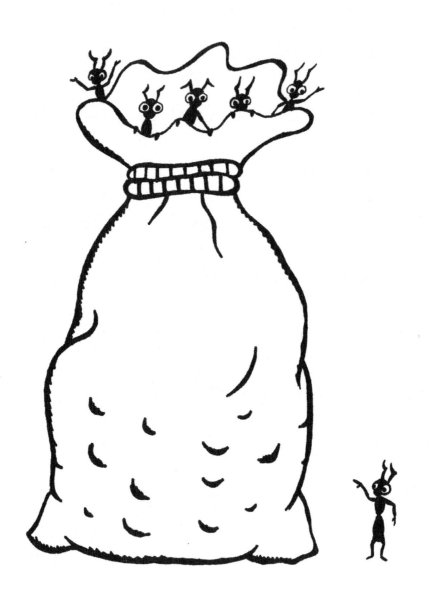

CONTROLLING YOUR ANTS

Now that you know about your greatest asset, your brain, let's talk about your thoughts, which seem to come from your brain. Remember from the first chapter that *thoughts* are different from *feelings*, thoughts actually *generate* feelings, and thoughts are *automatic*. You might be wondering, if thoughts are automatic, where do they come from? What generates them?

Our thoughts actually come from many different sources. The strongest influences on our thoughts are 1) our family, 2) our peer group and our interactions with them, 3) our cultural background, 4) commercial media and social networks, and 5) life experiences—not in any particular order of impact. The order of impact, in fact, is different for each individual and depends upon the amount of time one is exposed to each of the influences and the strength of that influence (quality and quantity). For example, kids who spend a lot of time using screen technology will be more influenced by the media than those who read books more. Also, if you're playing violent video games rather than strategic, non-violent games, the messages you have roaming around in your head will be completely different.

Nonetheless, a combination of these influences gives rise to the thoughts we experience automatically or which seem to pop into our minds 24/7. Neutral or positive thoughts are generally not a problem; in fact, they can contribute to resiliency, good self-esteem, and an optimistic mood. As noted in the first chapter, all people, however, also have **automatic negative thoughts**, **or ANTs**, that can create undesired outcomes. Our goal with this book is to help you understand your personal ANTs, deal with them, and reset your brain for the life you want.

Family Influences: A family's values and styles of thinking and parenting affect children from birth. We all hear our parents and other authority figures tell us how to interpret events and see them living out examples of interpreting events. If Grandpa expresses the idea that foreigners are taking American jobs, for example, we may grow up holding his belief as well. If Dad thinks cats are creepy and always makes negative comments about

their habits and questionable hygiene, we may reach adulthood thinking cats are germ-ridden nuisances to be avoided. Get it?

It's normal and important, not to mention necessary, for families to pass on their beliefs and values to their children; groups of people have done so to ensure their safety and survival since time began. When you're a teenager and building the necessary skills for flying the coop and being independent, it's also normal to question whether or not your family's beliefs are your own. Interestingly, however, when under stress, humans have a tendency to revert to our earliest learning and think the automatic thoughts we absorbed long ago. Remember this! The fact can come in handy someday!

Peer Influences: As a teenager, you probably spend more time with friends than family. You're at school six to eight hours per day, and then after school you text, post on Facebook, Tweet, Snapchat, or whatever to stay in touch with your friends. In fact, many of your 70,000 daily thoughts are about your friends and what they are thinking and doing.

In fact, your brain is hardwiring you to look to your peers for approval and influence. It's a primitive survival strategy. You need to be valued by your "tribe," and you need to develop strong, supportive relationships, a "second family," so you're strong and independent enough to leave your "first family" when the time is right.

But, the opinions and values of your peer group influence your thoughts in both positive *and* negative ways. When friends come from varied backgrounds with experiences different from your own, your horizons can expand. Maybe your parents taught you that being gay was a bad thing, but some of your best friends believe being gay is no big deal. You might realize you think the same as your friend; the beliefs of your parents can give way to the beliefs of those with whom you identify.

Whereas peer influences are often positive, fixed and negative ideas and behaviors of your peers can encourage you to limit your own thinking. Peer mistreatment (AKA bullying), for example, challenges clear thinking and healthy brain functioning. If your peers reject and/or tease you without intervention—or get you to participate in treating others unkindly—it's inevitable you will develop many automatic negative thoughts. Your "Interpreter" is hardwired to record the mistreatment in order to form what can become permanent opinions about people, your worth, and social interactions in general.

Cultural Influences: Whether you realize it or not, the traditions, opinions, and beliefs of your particular culture and religion affect your thinking. One culture believes it's proper for women to keep their heads covered, whereas others believe females should dress as they wish. Some cultures think a certain food is undesirable, whereas other cultures value the same food. Some cultures tend to look at what is wrong with a situation, whereas other cultures are more  optimistic. Just as no culture is totally "right," no culture is totally "wrong" in its values. One thing is for sure, though: Cultural and religious values strongly influence the thinking styles of the culture's members.

Commercial Media and Social Networks: Social media such as Facebook and Ask.com, movies, magazines, video games, songs, and television all influence our thinking. Like families, movie or TV characters model how and what to think about scenarios and events. Most people spend time watching and reading things they basically agree with already, but sometimes you may be influenced by values and ideas not fully your own. The media's depiction of revenge, sex, love, emotions, and violence can form impressions you carry beyond the movie or the novel. Looking at models in magazines, for example, can lead you to exaggerate your own flaws and to tell yourself that the degree of airbrushed perfection shown is possible and desirable. Also, the images *missing* from the media can affect your thoughts as much as what is included. If the male action hero never cries or expresses fear, for example, we may decide these emotions are "girly."

Video games, too, have a huge influence on thoughts and moods. Although scientists are still divided about whether violent video games directly cause people to become more violent, the prevailing theory is that, while you are playing games and killing enemies, you are absorbing those violent images and they ultimately put you on edge, raise your aggression and anxiety, and make it more likely you'll lash out verbally or physically.

For your own benefit, you might want to track how your behavior with media helps or costs you. Having this information can only be of value. Information is powerful—and information about yourself is most powerful—because with it you have options, can make new decisions, or accept the results of your current choices.

Life Experiences: A final area that informs your thinking is your life experiences. If someone sexually assaulted you, you may have decided people are dangerous and unpredictable. If you were never chosen to play on a team at recess, you may think you are clumsy or less important than others. These personal events can leave you with unpleasant or traumatic memories. They usually shape your thoughts for a very long time. Severe trauma, in fact, can stay with you for a lifetime. If you have been abused or badly bullied in some way, changing your thinking will not be enough. You also will need the kind of support offered by

counselors, your doctor, or perhaps your pastor, rabbi, minister, imam, or teacher. The good news for big and small hurts in your past is that, by reflecting on your experiences using the tools offered in this workbook, you will be able to alter your thoughts and feelings about those past events.

TOP 10 COMMON ANTs

- Filtering
- All-or-Nothing/Black-and-White Thinking
- Overgeneralization
- Labeling
- Jumping to Conclusions
- Catastrophizing/Minimizing
- Personalization, or Taking Things Personally
- Disqualifying the Positive
- "Should" Statements
- Emotional Reasoning, or Believing Your Feelings

NOTICING AND CHALLENGING YOUR ANTS

The first step of challenging your ANTs is to recognize them and label each as an error in thinking. Noticing and writing them down can help you to pinpoint those contributing to a current struggle. Of course, many thoughts contain multiple ANTs, so keep that in mind. A brief description of each of the top 10 most common ANTs follows:

Filtering: You see a single negative detail and dwell upon it, to the point it colors everything. For example, you do poorly on a test right before the weekend. You can't stop thinking about your grade, and your mood grows dark. You can't enjoy the weekend, because it was "ruined."

All-or-Nothing, or Black-and-White Thinking: This is when you think in extremes—about yourself, others, or life in general. There's no gray area and no room for imperfection when it comes to how you see yourself or a situation. If anything about you is less than perfect, you're *all* wrong. This thinking pattern is the basis for unhealthy perfectionism. Because some failure is inevitable for everyone, perfectionism leads to believing you are a *total* failure. For example, an accomplished runner loses one race and tells herself, "That's it. I lost my edge." Then she decides to quit running.

Overgeneralization: You see a single negative experience as part of a never-ending pattern of defeat. For example, you don't get a job you want and tell yourself that you *never* get any breaks and *always* have the worst luck. The words *always* and *never* are good clues you are overgeneralizing.

Stereotypes are another form of overgeneralization. For example, if a blonde doesn't know the answer to an obvious question, then all blondes are "stupid."

Labeling: Extreme overgeneralization can lead to labeling people, including yourself, in negative terms, such as "I am a loser," rather than "Everyone fails sometimes." Any time you tell yourself, "I am a…," you are labeling yourself. We also label others negatively simply because we do not like them, their behavior, or their looks. But these are just thoughts with a mean or critical slant. They aren't "the truth" about a person. If you label yourself negatively, you will reduce your self-esteem. If you label another person critically, you will feel disgust, fear, or possibly anger.

Jumping to Conclusions: One example of this ANT is "mind reading." You decide you know the negative things someone else is thinking about you, without checking for accuracy. For example, you will not sit with a table of people in the cafeteria because you *know* they don't like you, even though you have no facts to support your thinking. This ANT can really take off when things go viral online! If someone posts a picture of you that isn't the most flattering or shares something you said or did, you can really assign a lot of thoughts to people before you even get a chance to check out the facts.

Another example of this ANT is negatively predicting the future. You believe you can predict how an event, or even your entire life, will turn out. You believe things will go badly, and you begin to feel as though they already have. This can even cause you to give up on things before you give them a fair try. Because your brain only lives in the now as far as feelings go, if you tell yourself that a situation is going to be bad, you will start feeling bad right now.

Catastrophizing/Minimizing: This ANT involves extreme thinking in one direction or another. Catastrophizing is when you exaggerate the importance of a negative event and make it into a real catastrophe. You may have heard of the analogy of "making a mountain out of a mole hill." You think small goof-ups are a big deal, like misspelling a word or saying something insensitive to a friend. A good sign you are doing this is when you use phrases such as "really, really terrible," "the worst," or "it will be awful." Let's go back to that unflattering picture of you that your friend posted. You think, "This is the worst thing that has happened to me! I can't believe she did this to me! I can't show my face at school tomorrow!"

Minimizing occurs when you downplay your own positive qualities. For example, you tell yourself that having good grades is no big deal or that it isn't important you worked hard and saved your money to buy a car. Minimizing is also when you make light of a bad experience. Some people minimize the impact of abusive treatment. If you're being bullied, sexually harassed, or dealing with a parent who is an alcoholic and you always try to shrug it off, you are minimizing.

Personalization, or Taking Things Personally: With the ANT "personalization," you see yourself as the cause of a negative event for which you are not responsible, or you interpret the actions of others as being caused by you. This happens in relationships. For example, your teacher is upset and you assume it's because of something you did. Or you spend Saturday baking a cake for a friend's birthday, and, when she tells you she can't eat chocolate, you feel very hurt and take it as a sign she doesn't value your friendship.

The flip side of personalization is **blame**. If it is not all about you, then it must be all about the other guy.

Disqualifying the Positive: With this ANT, when you're complimented, you find some reason to disagree. Also, you reject positive events and see them as out of the ordinary or weird. For example, you get great feedback on a paper and tell yourself, "Yeah, right. It would have been okay if I'd spent more time on it." Or your friend compliments your outfit, and you tell him, "No way. I look fat today."

"Should" Statements: You use thoughts of "should," "shouldn't," and "must" to motivate or punish yourself. This leads to guilt when it is about yourself, and anger and blame when you direct the statements at others. Common examples are: "I shouldn't be so fat." "I shouldn't be so needy." "I should be a better friend." "I should know all the answers to questions." "I should have the top grade." "I shouldn't have eaten those cookies." "I shouldn't bother my parents (teachers, friends, etc.) with my problems." "I should really call my friend like I said I would, but I want to watch my show. I'm a terrible friend . . . but she should know that I always watch my show on Tuesdays. Besides, she shouldn't be such a jerk and guilt-trip me when I say no!" The last example shows how quickly we can move from guilt to anger.

When "should" statements are about others, they sound like this: "People should know better." "They shouldn't treat me that way." "People shouldn't bother me. They should stay out of my way." These kinds of thoughts can lead to aggressive emotions and are common to kids who mistreat others.

Our brain decided that, in order for life to be fair, things should go a certain way. For example, we think, "Life isn't fair," but "fair" is an ANT! In truth, life is made up of what happens, some of it earned but most of it random. You probably picked up a lot of "should" from your family. Using "should" statements is a common way of expressing disagreement and unhappiness. But there are no universal "shoulds"! In fact, the seven billion of us on the planet all see things differently. We didn't all vote on how things should be.

Emotional Reasoning, or Believing Your Feelings: This thinking error stems from viewing an emotion as "reasonable." It's thinking that, because you feel something, it must mean it's the one and only correct feeling. Emotional reasoning often accompanies many other thinking errors. Many times, when people talk about their "gut feelings," they are describing their emotional reasoning. (e.g., "I knew it was right because I felt it was right.") Just because we feel an emotion doesn't mean it's necessarily true. It is our first feeling but not necessarily the right feeling about the situation. This isn't to say we should ignore our feelings and be androids. Instead, we can *be aware of our feelings and follow up with an examination of the thoughts that created those feelings.*

Why bother with noticing and challenging your ANTs? They affect your mood, which can then cause you to feel anxious, self-defeated, depressed, angry, jealous, and much more. Besides, you are thinking all the time anyway, so you might as well take control of your thoughts, your moods, and, ultimately, your life!

REALISTIC THOUGHTS TO THE RESCUE

Now to deal with your ANTs! In this workbook, we will be teaching you how to catch yourself in automatic thinking errors, to identify what kind of ANT it is, and to replace the ANT with a more realistic thought. To begin, you need to understand how automatic negative thoughts become problems. So, meet the **Negative Feeling Spiral.**

Events routinely take place in all our lives. Some are pleasant, and some are not. Most events are probably neutral. The ones we get excited or upset about are most likely more rare. An example of an event that may cause an ANT is having a difficult time understanding the information you're studying for a math test. The Negative Feeling Spiral starts when you think an unpleasant and distorted thought such as, "I'm never going to pass this test." Within five seconds of that thought, your body begins to experience feelings because of chemical reactions happening inside you. In this case, you might feel anxious, nervous, or irritated. If we draw it out, the Spiral looks like this:

NEGATIVE FEELING SPIRAL

EVENTS

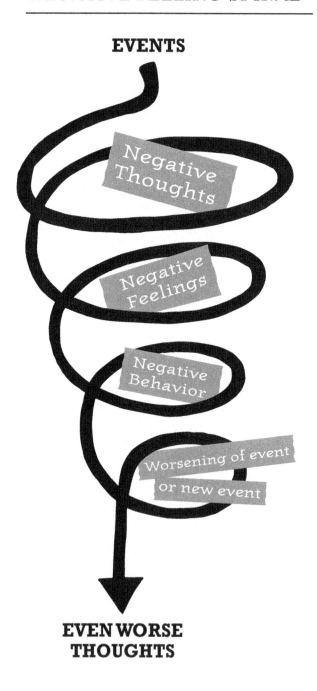

Negative Thoughts

Negative Feelings

Negative Behavior

Worsening of event or new event

EVEN WORSE THOUGHTS

Allowing the spiral to continue unchallenged creates a negative mood such as depression, low self-esteem, or anxiety. If you don't do something to stop it, you'll keep "feeding" your mood more negative thoughts, feelings, and events. Once you are in a negative mood, you will unconsciously gravitate toward activities that continue the mood and avoid those that would improve your mood. This is called **mood perpetuation**. If you are feeling down, you may sit and watch a marathon of reruns on television or scroll through hundreds of Instagram posts of someone's boring college trip, instead of going for a run or calling a friend to hang out. When you catch yourself doing this, you need to interrupt the spiral. You need to take a ramp off the ANT highway!

To interrupt the spiral, you can use **replacement thoughts**—realistic messages that disagree with the ANT. Replacement thoughts are balanced thoughts; they take the whole picture into consideration.

If you're sweating over a math test and also using this workbook, you might notice you were starting to feel anxious and ask yourself, "What was I just thinking?" Upon realizing you were jumping to the worst conclusions and telling yourself that studying was useless, you could replace the ANTs with the realistic thought, "This is hard. I'm not having an easy time understanding this. I need help. Is there anyone I can ask? I'm trying my best, but if I don't do well enough, I'm going to have to get help."

Realistic thoughts are balanced; they are objective, look beyond our ANTs, and reassure us that things are not all terrible. They are the things we would tell a best friend if he or she were having a similar problem. By consciously mustering realistic thoughts, you are basically learning to talk back to your **"inner critic."** Everyone has an inner critic that's a master of negative self-talk. Destructive, without value, and eating up a lot of time, negative self-talk can wear down self-esteem, make you anxious and depressed, and prevent you from thinking clearly.

When you challenge your ANTs, you silence your inner critic with thoughts that are self-accepting, and you begin to treat yourself like a best friend. This, ultimately, reduces your unhappy moments. Positive self-talk, in essence, is a balm and can help you to be healthy and happy.

Now that you are more aware (and hopefully convinced) that some thinking patterns are faulty and bad for your mental state, what should you do to correct them? For a long time, professionals who work with faulty thinking have taught their students and clients to practice a simple method to counter automatic negative thoughts. That method starts with noticing what you feel. Right! We're moving from thinking about *thoughts* to thinking about *feelings*!

Feelings indicate you have been thinking "mood-altering" thoughts. Even if you feel great, it's helpful to know how you got to those good feelings. That way, if you want to feel good, you will know the messages (thoughts) that make you feel better. When you notice you feel bad, it's a great time to examine what ANTs led to the unpleasant mood. Check out our "Box of Feelings." It may help you to identify the feelings with which you are struggling.

BOX OF FEELINGS

Exhausted	Depressed	Insecure
Mischievous	Overwhelmed	Sad
Disgusted	Suspicious	Bored
Hurt	Hopeful	Surprised
Frightened	Hopeless	Confident
Enraged	Angry	Shocked
Confused	Lonely	Anxious
Ashamed	Loving	Embarrassed
Cautious	Hysterical	Fearful
Ecstatic	Jealous	Proud
Shy	Envious	Happy
Smug	Frustrated	Confident
Guilty	Self-conscious	Peaceful

If what you feel is unpleasant and you want to change your mood, reflect on your thoughts and write them down. Here's a strategy:

1. Divide a piece of paper into three columns. In the first column, list your recent negative thoughts.

2. Look at the list of common ANTs. Then, in the second column, write down the ANT that matches/is causing each of your negative thoughts.

3. After you have gone through the whole list and matched/labeled each thought with an ANT, replace each ANT with a realistic thought in the third column. Remember, realistic thoughts are balanced. They are not overly positive, just true to reality. They put our shortcomings or the issues we are facing in perspective.

4. Do this until all your negative thoughts are addressed.

CHANGING MY MOOD WORKSHEET		
Negative Thoughts	**ANT Categories**	**Balanced Thoughts**
	SAMPLE	

Take a look at Zach's worksheet that follows. Zach realized he felt bad when he spent a lot of time on the bench during his football games. During one such time, he decided he was getting into a terrible and dismal mood, and he tried to turn around his feelings.

ZACH'S ANT WORKSHEET

Negative Thoughts	ANT Categories	Balanced Thoughts
All I do is sit here. I am such a loser. I don't know why I even tried out.	Black-and-White Thinking	I sit on the bench a lot, but what I do is valuable. I put in a lot of effort during practice. I'm supportive to the other players, too. Plus, I get some stuff out of this, like I'm stronger now from all this practice.
I fumbled that last play. I'm always messing up. I can't stand this anymore.	Filtering, Overgeneralizing, Emotional Reasoning	I don't always mess up. I got that clutch tackle in the last game.
I am too small to be a great player. We are always losing, and I'm probably causing it.	Personalization	I am small, but I am enthusiastic. The whole team is responsible if we win or lose—not just me.
I am making a fool of myself.	Labeling	I am not a fool just because I don't get a lot of playing time.
I should stop playing this game. I stink at football.	Should Statement, Emotional Reasoning	I could stop playing, but I think I would feel worse. I want to finish the season.
When coach said "good effort," I thought I would puke. He was patronizing me.	Disqualifying the Positive	Coach seems to mean it when he praises me. My heart is in the game.
I am never, ever going to live this down. People are going to hassle me.	Catastrophizing	It's not that big a deal. I'm making it bigger than it really is.

By the time Zach works through this process, he actually feels better because he has reframed his thoughts to be more balanced and realistic. He has broadened his view of the situation. Smart guy. Good thinking, Zach!

It's simple. You catch yourself in a downward spiral or getting all worked up, and you sit down and write a column of those mood-provoking thoughts. Then you identify the faulty thinking and label it. Lastly, you talk to yourself as you would talk to your best friend. Change the negative messages to balanced ones! Would you tell your friend he looks fat and ugly if he asked for your opinion? Probably not. You might be honest and say, "Yeah, you are heavier than you want to be, man, but I think you look good. You dress nice and usually carry yourself with pride. Keep it up. You're looking fine." Imagine talking to yourself with the same care and respect with which you try to treat your friends, *and you can imagine yourself in charge of your moods*.

In the chapters that follow, we will examine a number of common troubles such as anger, anxiety, self-esteem, and motivation. We'll show how ANTs create and contribute to our dilemmas, and we'll help you to practice identifying, labeling, and replacing the ANTs behind the problems.

And now for some follow-up work to make this information *yours*!

REST STOP

REMEMBERING
Key words and phrases: Can you define them?

Automatic Negative Thoughts (ANTs) _____

_____

Challenging Your ANTs _____

_____

Negative Feeling Spiral _____

_____

Realistic Thoughts _____

_____

Mood Perpetuation _____

_____

Inner Critic _____

_____

REFLECTING
Take time to ponder the following.

What values and opinions have you learned from your family, teachers, and other important adults?

_____

_____

_____

_____

_____

_____

What is your cultural background? "American" may be your nationality, but you're also from a particular culture even if your family has been here for 200 years. You have unique characteristics from your race, religion, political values, and ethnicity. What are the cultural values and beliefs that have shaped your thinking?

_____

_____

_____

_____

_____

_____

What life experiences have shaped your thinking? Have any events left you believing that certain people and situations are always bad, scary, safe, exciting, unsafe, dangerous, stupid, exciting, or wonderful?

_____

_____

_____

_____

In what ways do you see the media, especially social media, shaping your thoughts? What are the positive and negative media messages you have experienced? Which specific messages do you tend to believe?

_____

_____

_____

REINFORCING
Try these exercises to reinforce what you've learned.

1) Write down as many of the common ANTs as you can remember and give an example of each.

_____

_____

_____

_____

2) Create a sign that says, "Do I want to perpetuate this mood? What is it I'm really looking for?" Then hang it in a prominent place in your room. Use it as a reminder to challenge your thoughts when you're in a bad mood.

RECORDING AND RESOLVING

Journal writing is a great tool for learning how to control your thoughts and feelings.

Keep a journal of automatic negative thoughts for this week. This time, use the same format Zach used to identify and reframe your ANTs. Take a moment to think about the negative beliefs you hold about yourself, others, life, and opportunities and where they come from. Record those beliefs here.

_____
_____
_____
_____
_____
_____
_____
_____
_____
_____
_____
_____
_____
_____
_____
_____
_____
_____
_____

Remember:

EVENTS → INTERPRETATIONS → FEELINGS → ACTIONS

STOP TAKING THINGS PERSONALLY

Now that we've explored ANTs in general, we're going to take a closer look at one specific thinking error, **personalization**. When you react to others' actions or words as if you're the reason they're behaving a particular way, you are personalizing. You see yourself as the cause of a negative event for which you are not responsible, or interpret the actions of others as being about you. The opposite side of the coin from personalization is **blame**. With blame, instead of holding yourself responsible for every problem, you view others as responsible for your pain. In either case, when you're caught up in negative mental chatter about who's to blame, you lose sight of being in control of your own feelings.

Let's illustrate these concepts with a story. Selena is a conscientious, responsible 16-year-old who is dating Connor. Because she tries so hard to do things right, Selena is prone to personalizing negative events. Selena has a great group of girlfriends who usually hang out after school, but, now that she is dating Connor, she has less time for them. On one afternoon after school, Selena went to study with Connor instead of meeting up with her friends. She turned off her phone at the library and ignored the texts from her friends asking of her whereabouts. Later that night, when she got home, she found out that on the way home bullies had harassed her friends and left them very shaken up. Her friends weren't trying to blame her, but, of course, they said things such as, "Where were you?" and "Why didn't you call us?"

Selena not only felt upset for her friends, but she also was *convinced she was responsible*. The story racing around in Selena's mind was that, if she had only been there, the bullying incident would not have occurred.

Although Connor tried to talk Selena out of these thoughts, her mind went on to create many reasons the event was her fault: If her friends hadn't been waiting for her so long, the bullies wouldn't have crossed paths; if she had chosen to spend the afternoon with her friends instead of Connor, the event wouldn't have happened. Ultimately, Selena's blaming herself for her friends' misfortune negatively affected her relationship with Connor, and they broke up.

Selena had a way out. If she had known how to control her ANTs, she may have discovered she was "personalizing" and then made an effort to think about the situation in a balanced way. Instead of fixating on having made the "wrong" choice, she could have told herself, "I'm really upset about what happened to Sofia, Angel, and Melissa. I wish I had been there to help out, but my not being there didn't make it happen. Things happen. People can be awful at times. I feel sad for them, but the incident didn't happen just because I wasn't there. It was okay for me to be with Connor. In the future, I'll remember to tell someone I'm not going to show up, but my failure to do this didn't cause the situation."

Blame is a thinking error when we tell ourselves that someone else is "making us" feel badly. If Selena were another type of person, she may have reacted to her friends being upset as a personal attack on her and turned on them. She could have thought, "Stop making me feel bad about myself!" even if they were simply sharing their horrible experience. Had she blamed her friends instead of herself, she likely would have lost those friendships.

WHY DOES PERSONALIZATION COME SO EASILY?

Why is it so natural to take things personally? Although Selena took it a little far and let her over-grown sense of responsibility lead to a lot of anguish, all of us at some time or another tell ourselves that how others are behaving is about us.

Nothing could be more normal than concern that others accept us. For many years of human history, we had to pay very close attention to make sure we fit into other people's patterns and views of the world so we could remain connected to the tribe. Otherwise, we might be cast out into the wilderness, forced to try to survive on our own.

Today, however, getting shunned won't literally kill us. But we're still social beings by nature and can't help but pay attention to and be affected by the behavior of others. In fact, social stress can have deep and endur-ing negative impact on the brain. As a result, we sometimes assume another's response is about us or that some-

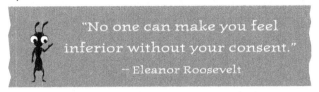

"No one can make you feel inferior without your consent."
– Eleanor Roosevelt

one caused us to respond in a certain way. But this is problematic thinking. In reality, as Eleanor Roosevelt said, "No one can make you feel inferior without your consent." In truth, people cannot *make* you feel a certain way; you always have a choice of how to interpret, act, and respond to a situa-tion. If you take personally the behavior of others, you will be flooded with the brain chemistry of anxiety, and you will respond in a state of emotion-al upheaval.

PERSONALIZATION AND ADOLESCENCE

Your teen years are a time of shifting moods, of experimentation with new behaviors, and of trying on new identities. Most of the time, the mood shifting and experimentation is harmless. Other times, however, you might take the new behavior of your peers personally and feel disappointed or angry. They might also take your changing behavior personally, too, and become angry at and disappointed in you.

Personalization is an extreme form of mind reading that derives from a mixture of sources. One source is our keen (but often incorrect) ability to read situations. Humans are biologically capable of deciphering one an-other's body language and **microexpressions**, those "telling" facial expressions such as raised eyebrows of disapproval, tight lips, and darting eyes—and then reading much into what we see. What we "see" in another comes from our pre-vious life experiences and the negative self-talk recorded in our brain's neuro-pathways.

Because acceptance from our peers is so important—not just to young people but to people of all ages—it's easy to be on hyper-alert for any signs that someone thinks we aren't "good enough." With the shifting moods in yourself and in your friends, the opportunities for personalizing another's behavior are boundless.

DON'T GET HOOKED ON OTHER PEOPLE'S OPINIONS OF YOU

One way of controlling the ANT of personalization is to not get hooked in the first place. **Getting hooked** occurs when you're jolted and react to someone's behavior from a place of *personalization*. To understand this concept, let's look at one scenario and two different reactions. A car speeds past people walking on a nice evening, and a teenage girl yells, "You suck!" out the window at different people she passes. Because all of us are different, with different life experiences and unique interpretations, this random act will impact individuals differently.

Jada was out for a walk with her dog when the girl passed. She simply shook her head and said to herself, "What a pathetic thing to do. I'd hate to be so angry." She then simply continued her walk, looking at the stars and thinking about an outfit she wanted to buy.

Kayla was also out for a walk when the girl yelled at her, but she had a completely different reaction. She yelled back, "You freakin' jerk!" then thought to herself, "I hate this stupid town. I can't even take a walk without some idiot hassling me. I hate the girls in this town. They're all rude. I've gotta leave this place."

In those two scenarios, who would you guess is taking the random event personally? The teenage girl yelling out the window didn't know Jada or Kayla, so whatever she said—positive or negative—couldn't possibly have anything to do with them. Jada didn't get hooked, so she was able to continue enjoying her evening. Kayla, on the other hand, ruminated all evening and was sent into a downward spiral of personalization and blame. She got hooked because the yelled statement reflected a negative belief she already had about herself and her environment. If Kayla didn't already believe she and her town "sucked," she would not have gotten hooked.

In some situations you may be treated poorly by someone you know, not a stranger. It's easier to learn to write off the poor behavior of random people and harder to break the habit of personalizing the actions of a friend. Let's look at a personal interaction that Jada and Kayla shared and how each reacted.

Both Jada and Kayla are juniors and have an average number of friends. One day, each of them greeted a friend in class, only to have her turn away and ignore the greeting. Jada was quick to personalize her friend's reaction. She thought, "Uh, oh! What did I do? I must have done something wrong." These thoughts troubled her until the end of class when she told herself, "I can't think of one thing I've done, so maybe it's something else. I'm going to see if she'll talk to me." Jada had started to take her friend's behavior personally, but she eventually caught herself, replaced her ANTs with a balanced thought, and responded by deciding to take action.

Kayla reacted differently. She immediately thought her friend was being a jerk. (Well, actually worse than a jerk, but this is a G-rated book!) She decided she wouldn't greet her again after class. She was blaming her friend for the slight, but she was still making it about herself. Kayla's interpretation (her ANT) was that her friend was behaving poorly because she intended to slight Kayla. Blaming another never relieves any stress. It's still a giant thinking error. Truth be told, both Jada's and Kayla's friends were in their own worlds having their own reality; it may or may not have had anything to do with Kayla's or Jada's presence.

In truth, there will be many times you will correctly assume that someone is judging you, rejecting you, or acting in a deliberate attempt to hurt you. These times will be unpleasant, but the treatment you receive is not personal. How someone else thinks, feels, and acts is about him or her, not about you or anyone else. Likewise, how you think, feel, and act is about you, not about anyone else.

Yes, all of us are capable of treating others poorly, but how we treat one another is all about what is going on inside of us . . . our turmoil, our good mood, our biases and prejudices, our pain, our good or bad self-esteem. Someone may want to hurt you, but that person's negative judgments are reflective of what's inside that individual, not what's inside you. And the same is true for you. What *you* see in a friend, peer, stranger, or even family member is about *you* and *your* relationship to the world, *your* mood, *your* value system, what is inside *you*, what *you* believe about yourself, and *your* personal framework.

To **project** on another (and we all do this) is to see in the other what is actually going on inside of us. This is a complicated concept and may take time for you to accept as true. Nonetheless, the nugget of gold we want you to hold onto is that, when people are unkind to you, they don't have x-ray vision that can see to the center of your soul. They are caught up in their own movie and along you come as a convenient "screen" to project their beliefs, reactions, and issues.

In addition, *you* do not have x-ray vision into the souls of others. You react to the mood inside and engage with others from *your* feelings, caused by *your* self-talk. If you recognize that what is said or done to you is the projection of the other person, then you can remember you are just his/her blank screen.

There will be many times you will know, or wonder, if you had any part in being treated poorly. The answer is that quite possibly you did. No one is perfect, and we all do unpleasant things to others. In these instance, if you catch yourself personalizing poor treatment, you might ask yourself what part of this uncomfortable treatment feels deserving. The next and very important step is taking the time to reflect on the part of the other's reaction to you that felt true and offer yourself some "feedback." What might you want to work on? Could you behave in a way that might make you feel more proud, more authentic? During this "feedback" reflection, be sure to stay both respectful and caring toward yourself. This reflection is the step in ANT control of sorting out the ANTs in order to reach balanced thinking. In your balanced thinking, you may realize you aren't a bad person, but you have played a part in the problem. After reflecting, you may discover you want to **respond** to the poor treatment versus just **react** to it.

REACTING VS. RESPONDING

How do we get to a state of *responding* rather than *reacting*? Reacting is based on a gut feeling that arises from real or perceived danger. Strong and quick reactions originate in the reptilian and limbic system parts of the brain. Remember our flight-or-fight discussion? Neither of these brain parts are concerned with accuracy! When we feel threatened, we lose track of our deep thinking and usually have a flood of ANTs that shout, "I did it!" or "You did it!" When we believe the threat without questioning our thoughts, our immediate reaction may be to throw a punch, yell, or swear, but often that behavior just alienates others and burns bridges.

Responding, on the other hand, takes time in order to calm down and gather our thoughts, analyze for ANTs, and engage when we reach balanced thoughts. Getting to a balanced response often comes after a "pause." Look at the process this way:

EVENTS → PAUSE/THINK → RESPOND

During the pause—which doesn't have to be more than a dozen deep breaths—you have time to engage your prefrontal cortex and make an informed decision on how to respond to a particular situation rather than reacting in fight-or-flight mode. Examples of thoughtful questions you might ask yourself during your pause to gain awareness are:
- What just happened that upset me? What was I thinking after it happened?
- What are the ANTs in my thinking and what balanced thoughts might be true?
- What response would be the most conducive to preserving the relationship I want with this person?
- How can I act in a manner that will support the best outcome for all involved?
- Should I get more information? Perhaps I don't know something.

Sometimes others say something that is both true and also meant to be mean or hurtful. But even if something is true, it's still important you choose what part feels accurate to you and what part doesn't. In fact, you get to decide not only *if* it's true but *how* it's true. Invariably, if you're having a strong reaction, it's because some part of what was said (up to 10%) does feel true to you. It's important you don't miss valuable information about yourself by looking only at the 90% that belongs to the other person and pushing it all away. In the end, you get to decide— using your frontal lobe and, consequently, your best thinking—what your response will be and what part of the information you will take to heart.

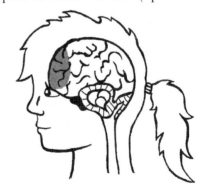

If your inner feedback is negative or challenging, it's not an invitation to your inner critic to host a "Bashing on You" party. Likewise, if the inner feedback is favorable, it's not an invitation to be defensive. You might merely use the information to strive to be emotionally healthier with more self-awareness.

THIS IS HARD WORK

Warning: Not personalizing a perceived rejection is really hard. When you don't get asked to the dance, win the student government election, or make the volleyball team, not attacking yourself or those you feel are responsible is challenging. When a person you find attractive  doesn't return your interest, not personalizing the rejection is tough. In the midst of your parents arguing over money, it may be difficult to keep from telling yourself you're a burden. If you've ever suffered from physical, sexual, or emotional abuse, avoiding self-doubt or even self-loathing can be very hard. And you may even blame yourself if your parents divorce or drink excessively.

All these examples are unpleasant experiences and can easily provoke the self-defeating beliefs lingering in our minds. But remember: They are unpleasant events, but they are *not* personal. You're not the cause of the negative experience; you may not even be a participant. If someone harms you through carelessness or intent, it's their poison, not yours. When you *change your negative self-talk*, you change how you feel. Remember that events don't create our feelings; our thoughts do!

Even good interactions can be, and often are, projections. For example, if you take it personally when a friend tells you you're cool, you assume you're cool simply because he/she says so. This may seem like a good thing, but it makes you vulnerable to being pulled down the minute that friend changes his/her mind.

This doesn't mean you shouldn't feel good about receiving a compliment. The point is: If you can maintain a strong sense of self, then you won't look to others to define you. You will know feedback is mostly a reflection of and about the speaker. With this perspective, a compliment can feel good, but a negative reaction will not ruin your day.

Of course, it's important to know how others perceive us, so we can look at the ways in which we can make positive changes in our relationships. When we understand the part of an interaction or struggle that is ours, we can more clearly ask for the behavioral change we need from the other person, and vice versa.

Rejection is a common occurrence in life, whether people mean to do it or not. It hurts, and, depending upon how big a rejection it is, the hurt can be significant. When we take rejection personally we make the hurt and disappointment worse. Small rejections, like the following example, are likely to happen throughout your life. How you view and respond to the disappointments of friendships will determine the moods you live with. Consider these two options in dealing with a typical relationship frustration.

Event Happens: Your friend Ciera breaks a longstanding plan with you to go out with a boy in whom she is interested.

Thoughts Follow: "Ciera cares more about that stupid boy than she cares about me. Maybe she doesn't even care about our friendship. Maybe she's embarrassed to be hanging out with me." (Personalization)

Feelings Follow: Disappointment, self-consciousness, insecurity, doubt, shame, disappointment, and loss.

Behaviors Follow: Withdrawal from peers, avoiding Ciera, playing hooky from classes you have with Ciera, skipping school, a downward spiral of negative thinking that causes depression.

This is how the situation goes for most of us. But what if you were working on your ability to not take things personally?

 ***Event Happens:*** Your friend Ciera breaks a longstanding plan with you to go out with a boy in whom she is interested.

After identifying that you are taking the event personally, you write down these replacement thoughts: "I am so disappointed. I thought Ciera was also really looking forward to the play. I wonder if someone else might go with me to the play. I need to tell Ciera the choice she made didn't feel good and that keeping plans is important to me."

Feelings Follow: Disappointment, a little frustration, peace, optimism.

Behaviors Follow: Talking to Ciera about the importance of keeping plans, calling another friend to see if I can still go with someone, entertaining the possibility of attending by myself, seeing if I can transfer the tickets to another night when either Ciera can go or someone else is available to attend with me.

Events like these occur on a daily basis, and the way we see them will either cause us to spiral downward into negative emotions or lead us to growth. When we have practiced reeling in and eliminating our ANTs and hold the clear awareness—and practice—of not taking things personally, then our interactions have a completely different quality. We also hold open the possibility for a new relationship with ourselves and with others.

REST STOP

REMEMBERING
Key words and phrases: Can you define them?

Personalization _____

_____

Blame _____

_____

Projection _____

_____

Microexpressions _____

_____

Getting Hooked _____

_____

Reacting vs. Responding_____

_____

REFLECTING
Take time to ponder the following.

Become an investigator on your own behalf using an exercise called mind mapping. It's a way to access your historical blueprint. Identify how you approach the world by identifying faulty assumptions and exposing ANTs. Complete the following sentence stems, and when you are done writing, go back and identify the ANTs that crawled out:

A. I will be valued or liked if I _____

B. You are valuable and likable if you_____

C. I will get what I need in life if_____

D. You will get what you need from me if _____

E. When I am angry, it's okay to_____

F. When you are angry, it's okay to _____

G. Happiness comes from _____

H. Sadness comes from _____

I. If someone values me, I will know by _____

J. When I value someone else, he/she will know by _____

K. Girls should _____

L. Boys should _____

M. When I make a mistake _____

N. If someone else makes a mistake _____

O. To be imperfect is _____

P. I would be defective if _____

Q. If someone knows I care about them, he/she will _____

R. I am successful when _____

REINFORCING

Try this exercise to reinforce what you've learned.

Cut out the shape of a heart and write on it in big letters, "PAUSE." Stick this PAUSE heart in a prominent place, perhaps on the cover of your school notebook, to remind you to take a deep breath, pause, and think before instinctively reacting to negative events or taking things personally. Practice "pausing" and then "responding" until the behavior becomes a habit.

RECORDING AND RESOLVING
Journal writing is a great tool for learning how to control your thoughts and feelings.

Review your answers to the sentence stems in the "Reflecting" section above, looking for common themes. Write them in your journal. They will help you to identify the core beliefs you hold. Then, journal about which of your core beliefs are supportive and help you to become emotionally healthier. Which are destructive ANTs you need to address?

_____

_____

_____

_____

_____

_____

_____

_____

_____

_____

_____

_____

_____

Remember:

EVENTS → INTERPRETATIONS → FEELINGS → ACTIONS

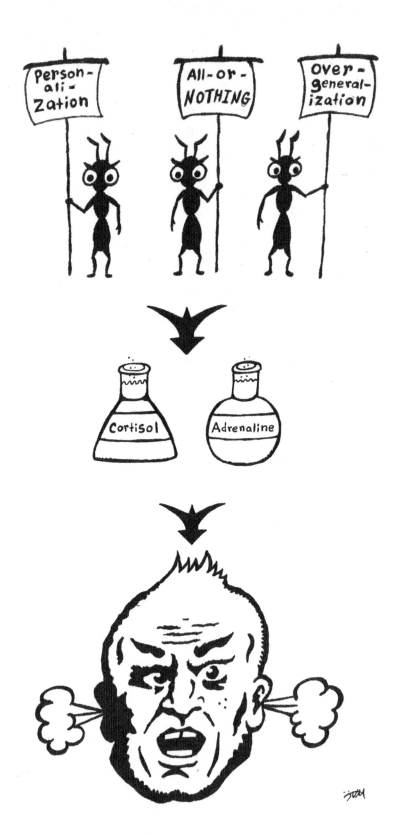

COPING WITH UNHELPFUL ANGER

We're going to suggest something you might think is outrageous. It's about anger. Here goes: *Other people cannot make you angry*. Rather, you become angry because of how *you interpret* an external event that's stirring up your emotions. We hope this news doesn't make you angry, because this is a really good thing! It means you can actually decide what or who you allow to push your hot buttons and how upset you will become. *That's real power!*

Of course, negative events occur, and they may disappoint you, offend you, or even seem horribly unfair to you (a thinking error, remember), but no matter how bad the event, your personal Interpreter decides how you view the situation and creates every single bit of anger and rage you feel. Remember the formula from the first chapter:

EVENTS → INTERPRETATIONS → FEELINGS → ACTIONS

Let's explore what happens in your body when you get mad. When you feel threatened for any reason, that almond-shaped set of neurons in your brain called the amygdala tells the small but mighty adrenal glands to release a squirt of adrenaline. Adrenaline tells the brain to send more blood flow to the lungs, heart, arms, and legs. At the same time, blood flow is restricted in the brain, especially in the frontal lobe area where you do your problem-solving. If you were in great danger and running from a mountain lion in the forest, the extra blood flow to the lungs, heart, arms, and legs would help you to run away. However, if you have high emotional arousal, you won't be able to think clearly to solve regular day-to-day problems because you won't be engaging your prefrontal cortex. Instead, you'll automatically pull out all your emotional and verbal fighting skills and go on attack with anger.

The good news is that your amygdala and your prefrontal cortex (thinking and problem-solving central) work together. Although the body's first reaction to perceived danger is always a stress response such as fight or flight, ideally the reasoning part of your brain eventually tries to figure out if the situation actually requires action. That's why it's so important to *check what you are thinking*! Are you jumping to a conclusion, or is there really a threat?

Many times we don't check our thinking. This can lead to becoming more upset and having more fight/flight/freeze chemicals released. If we keep looking for evidence that we should be angry, our brain will add cortisol and adrenaline to our bloodstream, causing an upset feeling so big it could go on for an extended period of time. So, it's pretty important to catch our anger early—and not make a mountain out of a molehill!

> **INTERESTING FACT**
>
> **The stress response in one's body can lead to meanness, messes, and misunderstandings.**

ANGER CAN COST US GOOD FEELINGS AND GOOD TIMES

For an example of how anger builds over small things, let's look at Maya's case. One evening Maya waited for her mom to pick her up for a quick trip to the mall. All she needed to do was run in for a pair of jeans, which she wanted to wear to school the next day. Maya's mom, a nurse, is often a little late because her shift doesn't always end on time, and she can't leave until things slow down. As Maya waited, she began to pace from window to window looking down the street for her mom's car. The more she paced and looked, the more she began to tell herself, "Isn't this just typical? I can't count on her for anything! Now what will I wear tomorrow? I have nothing! She makes me so mad. She never does anything for me." All the while, Maya is building up those stress chemicals like cortisol and adrenaline that make her ready to fight or flee.

With only an hour left before the mall closed, Maya's mom pulled up to the house and honked. Because Maya had chosen to tell herself a number of upsetting things and had all those stress chemicals in her system, when she slid into the car, she shouted, "Thanks a lot for ruining my evening, Mom!" This angry outburst gave Maya a short release but built up even more stress chemicals, meaning that was just the beginning of the explosion. Unfortunately, Maya's mom interpreted this external event poorly and did a little overreacting herself. What happened next was a huge blowout that kept both of them from going to the mall and left Maya grounded for the week!

Unknown to Maya, her mom had worked through her lunch in an effort to get off on time. Maya's mom knew she was still running a little late, and as she drove home, her tension increased as she anticipated her daughter's anger. Because of her own worry, Mom's fuse was short, creating a recipe for disaster. Could the situation, instead, have been an opportunity for connection?

It was a nerve-wracking wait and the jeans were important to Maya, but was the pain and suffering she inflicted on herself and her mom worse than being late to the store? Was it worth losing the shopping trip just to indulge her anger? For most of us, probably not. Let's picture a successful redo.

When Maya starts to feel angry as she waits for her mom, she tells herself to breathe slowly and listen to her thoughts. She has trained herself to recognize when her thinking is setting off unnecessary stress, and she knows *her interpretations and her ANTs* are stressing her out—not her mom's behavior. Although she prefers that her mom be on time, her rational mind knows that things happen outside people's control. When Maya breathes slowly and deeply, her brain tells her glands to stop sending out stress hormones and says to her body, "It's all good."

Maya catches her automatic negative thought, "Everything is ruined," and she chooses not to believe the story. Instead, she replaces that thought with a more balanced one: "It's disappointing, but it could still work. If it doesn't, I'll get the jeans tomorrow." Maya knows that, when she feels gratitude for the good things in life, things tend to work out better. Research shows that gratitude has a calming effect on the amygdala. People who report having high levels of grateful thoughts also report greater happiness and less depressed moods. Now that you understand that thoughts lead to feelings, doesn't this make sense? If you're focusing on how grateful you are, you will feel blissful, not blistering (Emmons and McCullough).

So when Mom pulls up and honks this time, Maya is only slightly anxious. She runs to the car and says, "Whew, I was worried. Can we still make it on time? I appreciate the ride." Mom smiles and nods, happy her sacrifice has been appreciated. And later, while they're at the mall, she mentions she earned a lot of overtime pay this week, so why doesn't Maya get that cute little blue top, too?

Hmmm... which scenario would you choose?

EVEN YOUR PARENTS DON'T MAKE YOU MAD

Many people find it difficult to believe they are creating their own anger. Media, fiction, cultural beliefs, and family attitudes can all convey the message that other people or events outside of us make us mad, but it's just not true. Anger is normal and natural, and it is manufactured by our minds. We see something, think something, and then feel something.

Common ANTs leading to anger are personalization (or taking things personally) all-or-nothing thinking, and overgeneralization. To see how this works, read about Dylan's problem.

Dylan is just like most people, easygoing at times and insensitive at other times. He isn't someone who would typically be considered a bully, but, when he takes an event personally, he often vents his hurt and anger on others. So, you might say Dylan is a part-time bully, not a full-time bully.

Likewise, on occasion, Dylan's dad treats Dylan in hurtful ways. His father can be harsh and strict and use words such as "stupid" and "idiotic" when he interacts with Dylan. Dylan never lets on he is hurt but often becomes enraged after a lecture from his dad. Sometimes the cortisol builds up so much in Dylan that he has an outburst of this rage, and his brother and other kids at school become his target.

Big emotional upsets or high emotional arousal (large doses of cortisol and adrenaline in your bloodstream) can cause ineffective actions and communication. The stress response in one's body can leads to meanness, messes, and misunderstandings.

On one unhappy morning, when his dad vented his frustrations onto him, Dylan left for school emotionally upset and in fight-or-flight mode. His father's harsh words (his ineffective communication) left Dylan thinking, "What a jerk my dad is. He doesn't understand me at all. I've had enough of his disrespect. He is never decent to me. Every time I mess up, he is all over me." The more Dylan thought about his anger at his dad, the higher his emotional arousal became. When he got to school, he was looking for a fight. All it took was noticing another kid having a good time while Dylan was in a bad mood, and Dylan attacked him with mean and nasty comments. He cursed at the boy and told him he better watch out for himself. He also made fun of the boy in front of other kids in the hallway. Because Dylan has a lot of friends, they laughed at the way he was acting instead of calling him on it.

Dylan actually felt a little better after he exploded at the other kid. This is because he released some of the pent-up chemicals. But he also found himself confused and a bit uncomfortable about his actions. He even thought his reaction was ridiculous, and that made him feel a little down.

It takes practice to remember we are always interpreting the events we experience, and that our interpretations are not 100% accurate. Dylan needed to take the time to test out his automatic thoughts and replace them with balanced thoughts. For example, remember the ANT of labeling? Labeling his dad a "jerk" was the first thing that started the "fight" chemicals flowing in Dylan's brain.

It's very hard not to personalize your parents' behavior, but, remember, others' negative actions aren't necessarily caused by you, so they should not be taken personally. In fact, Dylan's dad lost his job months ago and has been worried and down on himself. His short temper is less about Dylan than about his own frustrations in life. Although his dad isn't perfect, he often hangs out with Dylan, praises his athletic performance, and helps him work on his lay-ups. When Dylan thinks, "He is never decent. He always disrespects me," Dylan is engaging in all-or-nothing thinking and overgeneralization, both thinking errors that contributed to his angry outburst.

PERSONALIZATION AND BLAME CAN LEAD TO FURY

You have heard of tragedies and senseless violence carried out by emotionally disturbed young people who have personalized others' teasing and rejection. As we learned in the last chapter, many of us fall easily into the trap of viewing perceived or real rejection as a personal insult. We may believe others see something about us that is a reason for disapproval, or we decide that, even though they're wrong, they think they're superior.

It's natural to be upset over perceived rejection. In fact, anthropologists who study ancient humans tell us that in the Stone Age the worst thing a

tribe could do to an individual was to **ostracize** him/her, or leave the person out of tribal activities. It was a punishment worse than death to know you were now invisible to the people you depended upon for help gathering food and staying warm and safe. Scientists also believe

that the tendency to think negatively about rejection is hard-wired in our systems, and that we have evolved to think this way in order to survive. So, it's easy to understand why a cave dweller could "think his way to anger" about rejection and why we quickly think the worst when others seem to leave us out of their circle.

Sometimes we observe that others reject us, and that observation causes us to have the automatic negative thoughts that lead to anger and blame. We might *sense* people are avoid-

"Get curious, not furious."

ing us or find out someone hasn't invited us to an event. Whether real or perceived, *we can still choose* how we will respond to others' behaviors. When we think something is going on with our friends, we can check out the facts before deciding what to think. Information gathering is a great tool for ANT control! One psychologist suggests we learn to, "Get curious, not furious." This is good advice for *any* event that may trigger anger-causing ANTs.

Before you automatically get angry about being ignored or left out, you could ask yourself the following:

• "Did I do anything that may have led to my being left out?"

• "Does my attitude say I don't want to associate with this person or these people?"

• "Am I making myself invisible to them because I am afraid they will reject me anyway?"

• "Is there something going on that has nothing to do with me?"

• "Are these people simply not that friendly? Maybe this just isn't my group of friends and that's okay."

After the self-questioning, it may be time to be direct with your friends. Remember, be curious before becoming furious! Leveling with people about your perceptions and being willing to listen to their perspectives can cut down on misunderstandings.

> **"What I think, what I feel, and what I do is more about me than it is about you. And vice versa."**
> - 12 Step Program

However, you must keep in mind they will be sharing *their own thoughts and opinions* (not facts!) about your character or motives. It's important not to personalize what others think and feel. Although it's usually pleasant to be liked and unpleasant to be ignored, it's simply that: pleasant or unpleasant. It's not personally about you. You can do your best to be the person you like and you want to be, and still others may not see you the same way. That is just part of being a human. No one is universally liked.

Sometimes people do mean things to be hurtful. There are a number of reasons why. They may be **bigoted**, or stubbornly devoted to an opinion or prejudice. They may be emotional bullies, people who use verbal and physical aggression to make others feel disrespected. This can be done through gossiping, name calling, threats, intimidations, rumor spreading, or negative posting on a social network. Or they may fear rejection, so they reject you first.

When someone is being mean, we can choose to view the insensitivity, cruelty, or rudeness as that person's attempt at self-protection or his/her problem. A saying from the 12 Step Program for recovery from substance abuse goes like this: "What I think, what I feel, and what I do is more about me than it is about you. And vice versa." This is an example of a balanced viewpoint and one that won't lead to thoughts of anger, blame, and retaliation.

Regardless of whether others are intentionally trying to hurt you or you jumped to an incorrect conclusion, you need to be in charge of your own self-esteem. How you view yourself must be a product of healthy self-acceptance and your own critique of your success at living up to your standards. Yes, what others think of you is important, but it can only be one factor in forming self-opinion. Your job is to be the best you that you can be. Your job isn't to form yourself entirely to please others. Holding on to your faith in yourself is crucial to having clear thoughts and a stable mood.

Also, if you are bullied, it's important not to take it personally. Let's look at the facts about bullying:

- Nearly 1 in 3 students (27.8%) report being bullied during the school year (National Center for Educational Statistics, 2013).

- 19.6% of high school students in the U.S. report being bullied at school in the past year. 14.8% reported being bullied online (Center for Disease Control, 2012).

If this many students are being bullied, it shows us that bullies are picking on people whom they believe they can get away with bullying. We also know that:

> Stand up, step in, and speak out. Get caught doing the right thing: STAND FOR COURAGE.
>
> www.standforcourage.org

- 64% of children who were bullied did not report it; only 36% reported the bullying (Petrosina, Guckenburg, DeVoe, and Hanson, 2010).

- More than half of bullying situations (57%) stop when a peer intervenes on behalf of the student being bullied (Hawkins, Pepler, and Craig, 2001).

Don't be afraid to get assistance from adults if you need it, and, if you notice someone else being bullied, you can help by helping that person to get away from the situation or tell an adult. Perhaps the most important thing you can do after someone is mistreated by another is to spend time with that person, listen to him/her, and just be a friend (Davis and Nixon, Youth Voice Research Project, 2013).

STOPPING YOUR ANGER IN ITS TRACKS

Now that you realize your anger is the emotional result of your pesky ANTs, wouldn't you like to move past anger as quickly as possible and get back to feeling good? Given that the anger cocktail of cortisol and adrenaline can stay in your bloodstream for hours, it's good to have a plan for how to stop the feeling once it starts.

- Do something physically active. Go for a walk or a run, shoot some hoops, dance, do yoga, or get up and clean your room.

- Turn off the screens and be present with how you feel. No matter how distracting and entertaining our screens can be, we still need to get in touch with how we feel in the moment. If we don't know how we feel and listen to our thoughts, we can't own our minds and change our lives.

- Breathe. Sit down and put your hands on your knees, close your eyes and inhale to the count of four, hold your breath to the count of two, exhale to the count of four, pause to the count of two and then repeat. You will trick your gullible brain into thinking everything is okay. Once your brain believes everything is okay, you will calm down.

- As always, use your pen and paper to write down your angry thoughts and look for the ANTs. Label the ANTs and replace them with balanced thoughts.

- Now decide if there is any action you need to take. Don't react or respond to the issue that is triggering your anger until you are no longer angry.

REST STOP

REMEMBERING
Key words and phrases: Can you define them?

Ostracism _____

_____

Bigotry _____

_____

Personalization _____

_____

Balanced Thoughts _____

_____

REFLECTING
Take time to ponder the following.

How has your anger worked for you in the past? What positive things have come from your expressions of anger?

_____

_____

_____

How has your anger worked against you? What are the costs?

_____

_____

_____

_____

Have you ever become angry after being left out by others? Did you test the reality of your thoughts? What was the event, and how did it turn out?

_____

_____

_____

Have you ever been bullied? Have you bullied another? Have you witnessed bullying in person or online? What kind of thoughts did you have about the bullying? Are there any ANTs in that thinking?

_____

_____

_____

REINFORCING
Try these exercises to reinforce what you've learned.

1) Reread Maya's story. List and label her faulty thoughts.

_____

_____

_____

_____

_____

2) Watch a movie and observe how anger is portrayed. Do the characters get angry based on thinking errors? Does the movie justify the character's anger, or does it point out the ANTs driving the anger?

_____

_____

RECORDING AND RESOLVING

Journal writing is a great tool for learning how to control your thoughts and feelings.

Track your angry feelings this week. Record the thoughts that led to your anger. Label each ANT and write down a balanced thought for each one.

_____
_____
_____
_____
_____
_____
_____
_____
_____
_____
_____
_____
_____
_____
_____
_____
_____
_____
_____
_____

Remember:

EVENTS → INTERPRETATIONS → FEELINGS → ACTIONS

MANAGING ANXIETY

A re fear and anxiety preventing you from becoming all you can be? These difficult emotions can rob you of many things including:

- the ability to take action,
- a feeling of belonging,
- the capacity to participate,
- and a desire to join with others.

In essence, fear and anxiety can interfere with living the full and wonderful life you deserve!

You may experience anxiety over what seems like small things such as feeling too shy to go to a dance, or over serious issues such as freezing up when you face a test. For some people, anxiety can become so extreme that they are unable to drive a car or cross a bridge without experiencing panic. However big or small your problems with anxiety, they can stand in the way of your fully showing up in your life.

Anxiety and fear occur when your automatic negative thoughts (ANTs) trigger the natural "flight" instinct. As we mentioned before, all animals, including humans, are equipped with the fight-or-flight instinct. These instincts are biologically driven chemical reactions that occur naturally when presented with real or perceived danger. These reactions aren't only mental, but they're also physical and behavioral. When your mind registers danger, your body responds with an increased heart rate, quick and shallow breathing, muscle tension, and the increased production and delivery of the powerful stress hormone adrenaline. Then your inner cave dweller responds to the perceived danger with aggression (fight) if the odds seem in your favor, or by retreating (flight) if not.

Fear exists to move us out of harm's way. If it sounds like an important instinct, that's because it is. But there's a catch! We no longer live on the plains where wild animals and hordes of other cave dwellers are jumping out from behind every rock. In the modern twenty-first century, most of us live relatively non-threatened existences. Instead, we live in a world with *some* occasional real dangers but many more *perceived* dangers.

Our fight-or-flight instinct is still valuable for responding to those instances when we're truly threatened, but ANTs also take over and cause unnecessary fear reactions in the realm of perceived danger. As a result, many of us view life through a filter that puts our "feeling self" back out there in the wild, facing a charging mastodon. It's this type of unnecessary anxiety we hope to help you learn to understand and control.

Granted, life today is not free of stress; in fact, many issues *are* cause for alarm: Terrorism, poverty, drug abuse, racism, sexual harassment, war at home and abroad, and a general uncertainty about what lies ahead all contribute to our individual and collective stress. Fortunately, humans are actually well equipped to deal with stress, as we are highly resilient beings.

The flight instinct can become a filtering system through which we view our lives. What tends to over-stress us is the filtering system that sees *far too many things as dangerous.* Our bodies simply do not know the difference between what is actually perilous and what our ANTs falsely sense or see as a danger. Once the body has responded to the "danger" (a reaction that takes about five seconds), we may feel and behave as though we actually are in peril even though we are not.

In this chapter, we will study the ANTs that create, exaggerate, or reinforce our stress-related problems. We will take a look at how ANTs contribute to worry and panic—two manifestations of anxiety—and explore how to develop resilience by replacing ANTs with a balanced perspective and through anchoring techniques that reverse trends of anxiety in the mind and body.

WORRY

Worry is one of the most common forms of anxiety. Typically, **a worry cycle** begins with an event or the anticipation of an event. Next are the automatic negative thoughts that interpret the event as dangerous. Some of the ANTs that commonly feed worry are jumping to conclusions, disqualifying the positive, black-and-white thinking, catastrophizing, and magnifying.

Within five seconds, these thoughts are followed by a feeling of anxiety, which then dictates behaviors that attempt to manage the anxiety. The behaviors driven by worry usually fall into the categories of fleeing or fixing—such as avoiding situations, running from situations, trying unnecessarily to fix situations, or repeatedly checking on the safety of others.

Take a look at Kim's worry cycle in the story below and see if you recognize anything about yourself.

Kim is a sophomore who generally does well on her math homework, but she often struggles with anxiety when it comes time for mid-terms or final exams. The event that triggers the start of her cycle is the announcement of an upcoming math test. She begins to focus on a *perceived negative outcome*. One aspect of worry is the tendency to make negative predictions about a future event, which is called jumping to conclusions. Kim jumps to a negative conclusion as soon as she sees the test date posted on the board. Kim tells herself, "The test is too soon. There's no way I can do this. I'm gonna fail. I know it."

Many individuals suffer from test anxiety. Test anxiety is such a real and common problem that people have full-time jobs helping students to practice the very techniques we will teach you. The anxiety that one will fail no matter how prepared or knowledgeable creates such a stress reaction that the test taker experiences an actual mental block while taking the test. Test anxiety stems from looking ahead and visualizing failure. Once you paint that mental picture and

look at it over and over, your body says, "Yikes. This is terrible!" and the reaction begins whether you know the information or not.

Once Kim expects failure, her body responds with physical symptoms. She feels an overall sense of nervousness and restlessness. She even has a hard time catching her breath. This is the physical part of the worry cycle. When Kim notices the physical symptoms, it sets off another round of ANTs. Now Kim tells herself, "I'll never get through this test without freaking out (jumping to conclusions). I cannot believe how stupid I am (labeling). I can just see it now. I will spend my life flipping hamburgers because I can't stop freaking out (jumping to conclusions)! If I keep going like this, I'll end up with a C in this class, at best, and I'll never get into a decent college" (catastrophizing).

With her physical anxiety symptoms mounting, Kim believes these feelings are 100% true and reasonable (emotional reasoning). Remember, once you see a situation as disastrous, your body follows along, sending out feelings *as though the disaster has already struck!*

By now, Kim is in a panic. Her body is ordering her to get away from the danger. Kim follows the order by telling herself, "I can't handle this. I have no skills to handle this stress (black-and-white thinking). I'm such a loser. I can't believe I freak out so much and ruin my life" (disqualifying the positive by negative labeling).

So Kim decides to avoid the whole situation that evening and sits down with the remote control, ready to block out reality for at least the rest of Tuesday night, if not for the rest of her life.

Along comes Kim's mom, Mrs. King, who immediately wonders why Kim is watching re-runs of TV shows when finals are a week away. It doesn't take Mrs. King long to turn off the television and ask why Kim isn't studying. By the time Kim has explained her need to obliterate reality (did we mention the bag of cheese puffs that has made its way into Kim's hands?), she has once again talked herself into another bout of anxiety. Mrs. King sees the distress her daughter feels and, being a loving parent, tries to calm her with reassurances. Let's listen in.

> *Mrs. King:* "Don't be silly, honey. You're too hard on yourself. I'm always so proud of how you do in school. You worry too much."
>
> *Kim:* "Yeah, right. Whatever, Mom. You don't know what an idiot I am." (disqualifying the positive).
>
> *Mrs. King:* "You just need to relax and tell yourself you'll do fine. You always do well."
>
> *Kim:* "I can't believe you're saying this! You always think I'm great. You think I'm a genius if I just pass. I doubt UCLA will think I'm great when I bomb Geometry (jumping to a negative conclusion). You're just making me feel worse. I can hardly breathe!" (blaming)
>
> *Mrs. King:* "I want you to get your math book out and start to work. You need to work harder, that's all. Avoiding it won't help. Get started."
>
> *Kim:* "Can't you see it's too late (black-and-white thinking). I'm a loser (labeling). I just fall apart, and then I can't remember anything. It's hopeless." (catastrophizing)

."Okay, let's leave this scene before Mrs. King begins to agree with Kim—and they grab another bag of junk food and both escape to the island on *Lost*. What we need to do now is help poor Kim stop her avoiding behavior and start resolving her anxiety.

If you're someone who worries, feels a sense of panic, and then reacts by avoiding the issues frightening you, then the way out of your anxiety lies in tackling your ANTs. You'll need to 1) meticulously assess your automatic negative thoughts, 2) deliberately replace them with realistic thoughts, and 3) brainstorm the resources that could help you with your specific situation.

In the story above, Kim could sit down with a piece of paper and force her mind off the endless worry cycle and on to examining the thinking errors leading to her panic. After identifying those ANTs, Kim would be able to come up with coping options and form a realistic prediction of the outcome. However, before she picks up the pen and paper, Kim needs to relax.

Relaxation can be broken down into:
- Breathing
- Focusing Thoughts in a Positive Manner
- Doing (or Action)

Breathing: Breathing is the main key to relaxation. Think back to our cave dweller. When the fight-or-flight instinct kicks in, our quality of breathing is seriously affected. We would normally either stop breathing for a few seconds or take quick and shallow breaths. *When you notice your mounting anxiety, you can immediately check to see how you are breathing.* Gaining control of the way in which you are breathing in a moment of unease *can immediately eliminate 50% of your anxiety.* When you replace shallow breathing with **deep belly breathing**, you *reverse* the physical aspect of the process of anxiety. Okay…let's deep belly breathe. Yes, right now. We want you to stop what you are doing (reading this book, presumably) and try this technique. Wait! Read the directions first, and then experiment.

DEEP BELLY BREATHING TECHNIQUE

1. Sit comfortably with your hands resting lightly on your abdomen.

2. Close your eyes and take a few slow breaths—in through your nose and out through your mouth—that make your belly rise on the inhale and lower on the exhale. This is a "belly breath."

3. Breathe in to the count of four, hold your breath to the count of two, exhale to the count of four, pause to the count of two before you repeat.

4. Once you repeat this cycle for 2-3 minutes, notice how you feel. If you are still tense, then repeat the process.

You may be wondering why deep belly breathing works to calm you down. This form of controlling anxiety is standard equipment in the human body. Perceived danger tells the body to produce and secrete more adrenaline. Quick breathing tells the body to keep the adrenaline coming in order to actually run away from danger. If we are facing real danger, then we might need that reflex to kick in and help us to flee the situation. Once we escaped, we would sit down and catch our breath, which would signal to the body that the danger has passed.

When the danger is imagined and we just keep breathing quickly, our thoughts signal the body to continue sending out stress hormones so we can swiftly flee. Deliberately controlling our breath is one way to tell our body to relax; there's no reason to panic.

Focusing the Thoughts: Let's check back on Kim. By taking a break and doing a round of belly breathing, she made an attempt to control her anxiety. We are happy to report it worked well enough that Kim can now move on to the second component of relaxation: *focusing her thoughts.*

With some help from Mom, Kim sits down with a pen and paper and divides it into four columns: What I Fear, ANTs, Type of ANT, and then Realistic Thoughts. She starts by recording what she's anxious about under the column called "What I Fear." Then she records the ANTs and the thinking errors feeding these fears and labels each of them. Finally, she

counters the ANTs with realistic thoughts that help her to calm down and to cope with the anxiety in a proactive way.

Peeking over her shoulder, let's take a look at what she wrote:

What I Fear	ANTs	Type of ANT	Realistic Thoughts
I'm afraid my fear of tests will make me flunk my math test.	I just can't take tests.	Black-and-white thinking	I'm afraid of testing, but sometimes I do pretty well. I have a high B average, so I must do okay some of the time.
I'm afraid I'll never get over this stupid, stupid problem.	I'm stupid.	Filtering, Labeling	I'm not stupid. I'm an A and B student, and I couldn't do this well unless I was smart. I just get anxious sometimes and lose it.
I'm afraid I'm crazy.	My future chances are all ruined.	Jumping to conclusions, Catastrophizing,	This test won't really ruin my future. Like Mom says, "If this won't matter a year from now, don't sweat it." It won't matter a year from now. It's just a math mid-term; it's not a terminal illness.
I'm a failure.	I always screw everything up.	Filtering, Over-generalization	I probably won't fail the test. I've never failed one. I get nervous and make mistakes, but maybe if I breathe and go slowly I won't panic.
I'm a phony. I'm not really okay.	Everybody knows I'm "psycho."	Mind reading, Filtering	I have no idea what other people think. I don't want to be ruled by others' opinions.
I have to be perfect.	Mom says a B is a good grade, but I could never accept a B.	Black-and-white thinking, Disqualifying the positive	I don't have to be perfect; no one is. I will survive getting a B. If it happens, I can move past it.

Kim is feeling better already, so it's time to turn the paper over and develop a plan for coping with the anxiety. Here Kim can brainstorm ideas that will help her relax and make different choices instead of avoiding her challenge and staying marooned with the survivors of Oceanic Flight 815!

- I can ask the teacher for an old math test I can use for practice.
- I can go online and find practice geometry problems.
- If I panic during the test, I can use my belly breathing.
- I will use breathing any time I start to get anxious.
- I can go for a run or a bike ride every day because it helps prevent my panic.
- I can spend time picturing myself getting through the test with a good grade.

Doing (or Action): What Kim was experiencing is called **anticipatory anxiety**. As she imagined something coming up, she became extraordinarily worried. This happens to many individuals when they face tests, public speaking, parties, asking someone for a date, or applying for a job. Working on changing the thoughts that fuel anxiety is a key component, but, in most cases, action is also required. Sometimes we may wish all we have to do is change our thinking, but realistically we need to change our tactics more often than not if we are to tackle anxiety. So Kim is not only going to work hard on breathing and ANT control, but she also is going to use a proactive technique called **storyboarding** to get through her test anxiety. And, of course, she is going to study for the test!

Storyboarding is a tool filmmakers use when planning a movie, but it also can be an effective technique to help people change how they feel or how they act. People use it to overcome their fears of making speeches, as a tool for weight loss, and as a performance enhancer for athletic training, just to name a few. If you suffer from anxiety or panic, it may seem to you these kinds of tools are pretty small weapons to use on a very big problem, but actually they're the most researched, trusted, and tried-and-true treatments.

For an example of storyboarding, let's go back to Kim, who has been using her computer to study Geometry and has stopped because she is feeling a little anxiety coming on.

The first thing Kim is going to do is, you guessed it, belly breathing. Once that necessary step is out of the way, she is going to pull out her pencil and paper and rewrite the script of how she sees herself responding during her test. Before she can rewrite the script, she will need to be clear on what exactly makes her anxious, so she will begin with writing out the events she fears will happen. Here's what she wrote:

I wake up in the morning after not sleeping most of the night, and I immediately dread the day ahead. Yuck! I feel terrible. My palms are sweaty, and I feel all nervous, like I had two lattes before breakfast. I get to school, and all I think about until third period is how badly I am going to freeze up on that test. When third period comes, I go in there and get so nervous I can't understand anything I read on the test. I can't even remember how I did any of the practice problems. I sit there for 45 minutes and read and re-read the questions and maybe, by pure luck, get a few of them right. Then I leave class and think about nothing else but how I failed. I feel sick to my stomach all day.

In her story, Kim was very specific about the aspects of the test that will make her anxious as well as how that anxiety will feel in her body and how it will affect her performance. Next, she will re-write the script with the specifics of how she will cope with the situation in order to alleviate the anxiety. Note that she does not write a script in which there is an absence of anxiety; she writes one in which she prevails over the anxiety by using her tools.

I go to bed the night before the test at 9:30 and read a novel I enjoy for about 30 minutes. Then I am too sleepy to stay awake any longer. I usually don't go to bed until 11:30 or so, but I know the test is stressful for me and I want to get as much sleep as I can. I awake in the morning, and, although the first thing I think about is how scary the test will be, I get right out of bed and do my belly breathing before I even take a shower. During my shower, I just keep practicing in my mind how I will stay relaxed. I rehearse breathing and focusing, and I also envision myself stopping the ANTs when they start up. After my shower, I get a ride to school from Dad, and I talk to him about how well I have prepared for the test. I stay focused during first and second period on the class I'm sitting in, and, when my mind wanders to the test, I breathe and focus on the moment

I'm in. When third period comes, I walk to the math room, and I calmly sit down. When the test is placed on my desk, I breathe and reassure myself I have done so well on the practice tests and the homework that all I need to do is relax and stay confident. A few times the ANTs arrive, but I talk back to each one, and I use my belly breathing when I feel the anxiety coming. I complete the test on time, and I leave class feeling great about myself. I am awesome!

Kim's efforts to relax, to focus her thoughts, and to storyboard paid off in the weeks ahead. Before her mid-term, Kim looked at "worry control" as another homework assignment she needed to do every night. She had swarms of ANTs to contend with, but she worked to banish them and to replace them with realistic thoughts each time she noticed anxiety creeping up. When mid-term day arrived, she experienced about 25% of the anxiety she normally felt. She scored 92% on the test, and, although she was happy with the grade, she was thrilled even more by the success of her relaxation methods.

Noticing our negative thoughts and replacing them with a realistic picture takes a lot of effort and practice. But, hey, we are always thinking anyway, so we may as well take control of our thoughts, and, therefore, our moods!

HARLAN AND CHECKING BEHAVIOR

Besides avoidance like Kim experienced, another bothersome response can come from worry. The story of Harlan, which follows, illustrates how the cycle of worry also can lead to **repetitive checking behavior.**

Harlan has a girlfriend named Aria who likes him just as much as he likes her, which is quite a bit. However, poor Harlan is plagued with insecurities about their relationship of eight months. When Harlan is insecure, he begins to ask Aria if she loves him, and she generally assures him of her affections. The trouble is that this behavior only serves to reinforce Harlan's worry and fuels the cycle.

The triggering event of Harlan's fretting is often his "observation" that Aria "seems" distracted or distant. It doesn't immediately occur to Harlan she may be thinking about school stresses, be preoccupied with family issues, or be responding to any influence other than him. If Harlan texts Aria and doesn't hear back immediately, he always assumes something has changed in her feelings about him. Could it be Harlan is making everything *about him*?

He is quick to think, "She must be mad at me" (jumping to conclusions or mind-reading). He continues the cycle with, "She did seem kind of mad at me today" (magnifying or seeing disaster). "What did I do to get her mad" (personalizing)? "I'm always messing up. I know I'm gonna lose her for good" (black-and-white thinking and catastrophizing).

When Aria calls Harlan, the first thing out of Harlan's mouth is a reflection of his need to check and see if she is still there for him: "Aria, is everything okay? I've been going crazy." Aria briefly reassures him and then attempts to tell him about the unpleasant things that detained her, including being rear-ended at a stoplight, but Harlan keeps interrupting to check on his security. The compulsion to reassure himself against perceived loss overtakes his interest in Aria's real situation.

Well, we won't even go into what effect this has on Aria. Suffice to say that Aria is acting more frustrated and less loving as the conversation continues. Soon she will begin to actually feel distant from Harlan, and the cycle will begin again. Poor Harlan did not even get any value out of his attempts to reassure himself through checking, and he will ultimately drive Aria away.

Okay . . . poor Harlan needs a second go at this one! If you're a worried, reassuring type, you don't need any more action on the checking front. You need to learn to relax and do a little ANT control! So, after talking with Aria, Harlan finds a quiet spot and spends three minutes doing belly breaths. Then he gets out a pen and paper, ready to sort out his ANTs. On the paper, Harlan makes three columns. In the first one, he writes down all his negative thoughts. In the second column, he labels each thought as to which ANT is present. In the third column,

he writes down balanced, calming, and realistic thoughts. After 10 minutes of *reassuring himself,* Harlan is ready to call Aria back and to refrain from his worry-driven behavior. When Aria answers the phone this time, she hears, "Hey, Aria. How're you feeling? I thought you might want to talk about your lousy day, sweetie." Way to go and keep that awesome girl in love with you, Harlan!

SOCIAL MEDIA ANXIETY

The desire to constantly check your Facebook or Instagram can be as out of control as Harlan's need to keep checking to see if his girlfriend still likes him. Even if no one is actively putting you down online, you can still be anxious about missing something important, being left out of events, getting "likes" for your posts, and comparing yourself to the image people put out about themselves. Other people's posts can affect you negatively when you begin to have unchecked automatic negative thoughts about how you measure up, how popular you are, or your value. It's easy to forget that, like you, others post happy pictures, their real or made-up accomplishments, and comments that put them in a good light. If you forget this, you can begin to worry that you are inferior, deprived, or excluded. What is meant to connect us more (and technology can) makes us feel further apart. It's also easy to become shallow because you fear judgment and, instead of being real, you show only the side you think others will approve.

DEALING WITH A BULLY

Another common cause of anxiety for teenagers is bullying. You can be mistreated at school, at home, online, or even within yourself! It can make you feel unsafe, both physically and emotionally. In dealing with a bullying situation, you need to revisit the "personalization" ANT. Remember this quote? "What I think, what I feel, and what I do, is more about me than it is about you. And vice versa." This is a good phrase to keep in mind if you're dealing with a bully.

When you can stop your tendency to take personally the cruelty of someone mistreating you, it's like wearing a Teflon coating: Nothing will stick! Granted, it's really challenging not to take it personally when someone mistreats you, especially because bullies usually harass others about appearance, body build or size, and race—very personal attributes. Like the rest of us, you can sometimes be insecure about the "package" that is you, so your outer appearance makes an easy target. We all want to be accepted—and bullies strike at the heart of that vulnerability. You just have to remember to let the mistreatment slide off! The bullying isn't about you!

Rather bullies are coping with their own issues. They're more likely to have over-reactive rage/fear systems, and brain scans of people who engage in violent or impulsive behavior show that activity is centered in the lower brain, linking back to that inner cave dweller. When the lower brain is "in charge," the bully doesn't have access to his/her "higher" or rational brain, which would help him/her to problem solve. The result can be a lack of concern for others—or themselves!

If you are being bullied, it's normal for the mistreatment to cause you anxiety, and the long-term effects on you can be serious. The terrible experience affects your brain by creating and enhancing an overactive fight-or-flight and stress response, making you more likely to respond with anxiety and fear to even neutral situations. In fact, the impact of bullying has many similarities to Post-Traumatic Stress Disorder, or PTSD. This is the disorder that many war veterans come home with after dealing with the stresses of the battlefield. If you're badly bullied, you may experience problems with sleeping, eating, breathing, headaches, and other physiological symptoms, as well as avoidance behaviors, feelings of helplessness, and even thoughts of suicide. Suicide from bullying is a growing problem and such a big problem it has been given a name, "bullycide."

Standing up to a bully can be difficult, but you can protect yourself by being aware of the ANTs being caused by the situation. The bully's words and actions are a reflection of him or her—not you! Instead of taking the words and actions personally, seek the help of a trusted adult—a parent, a teacher, a coach, or a guidance counselor. You also can get help from friends. You can even make a pact to back up each other in these types of situations. Of course, your safety is most important. If you feel threatened in any way, by anyone's behavior, seek the help of an adult immediately.

BULLYING ONLINE

Cyberbullying is an increasing problem, rising to an epidemic level. Reports indicate that online bullying can be much more difficult to emotionally process and resolve than face-to-face bullying. What happens is that anonymity creates a situation in which others can join in the taunting without consequence. The target can't be aware if others would come to his or her aid, because the target can't see the empathy or outrage in the faces of bystanders. Lastly, cruel comments and taunting can be pervasive if they aren't removed from the Internet by authorities (Family Institute of Northwestern University).

In short, fear of being dissed online can create a great source of anxiety. Let's take a look at how Alexis dealt with a cyberbullying experience she encountered.

When Alexis broke up with Ryan, he became really angry. He created a Facebook page under her name and started posting threatening and cruel comments about her. He even posted a sexually suggestive photo she had shared with him when they were together, along with her email address and cell phone number. When he saw her at school, he shouted nasty insults at her, and his friends joined in and laughed.

Alexis felt humiliated! Her first reaction was to blame herself for Ryan's behavior: "It's my fault he's so mad; I should never have broken up with him" ("should" statement). She felt anxious all the time, waiting for the next cyber-attack. She was ashamed of the photo he shared and the name-calling, and she was afraid her life would be over if her parents saw the fake Facebook page (jumping to conclusions, catastrophizing). She even started to believe some of the things Ryan and his friends were calling her (taking it personally, labeling).

Thankfully, Alexis decided to seek the help of Mrs. Taylor, a guidance counselor at school. Mrs. Taylor helped Alexis recognize the thinking errors she was making: Ryan's behavior wasn't her fault. His actions said more about how he was feeling than about her behavior while they were dating or when she broke up with him. Ryan was also brought in to the office for disciplinary action.

Mrs. Taylor encouraged Alexis to ask her friends for help, so, the next time Ryan and his buddies decided to gang up on her in school, she had a support group to help her get through it. Alexis felt more confident; she was able to calmly tell Ryan to stop and to walk away. The taunting still hurt, but remembering not to take it personally made it easier to deal with. Eventually, Ryan's friends became more ashamed by their behavior, and Ryan did it less and less.

Mrs. Taylor also helped Alexis to get the fake Facebook profile, photos, and insults removed from Facebook by reporting the fraudulent activity, and her friends kept an eye out for anything Ryan posted on her real Facebook profile to ensure that any insults would get marked as spam and come down quickly.

Taking action against a bully isn't easy to do alone, so don't be afraid to seek help, like Alexis did. Mrs. Taylor helped her to muster the courage to find more support and stand up for herself, and the result was a stop to the behavior so Alexis could go on living her life—and find a new boyfriend who would treat her right!

PANIC

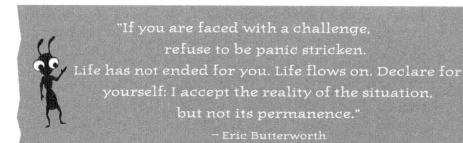

"If you are faced with a challenge, refuse to be panic stricken. Life has not ended for you. Life flows on. Declare for yourself: I accept the reality of the situation, but not its permanence."
— Eric Butterworth

Another form of anxiety is **panic**. Worry tends to be about outside events, whereas panic is focused inward and preoccupied with physical symptoms. Worry may trigger panic, but panic is concentrated on the body's physical response. Panic involves symptoms of the **flight reflex**. You might have a pounding heart, difficulty breathing, and start to sweat; in addition, you might feel numb, dizzy, or detached and "out of the body." All this occurs because the blood supply to your brain is decreased. Instead, the blood is being sent to your large muscles so you can run. However, the increased blood supply to your legs can make you feel wobbly, and the decreased flow to your hands can make them feel numb.

The important thing to remember is that these symptoms are *tempo-rary*. They are harmless, cause no bad effects on your body, and will soon subside. Once a person begins to panic, the experience or thought that has triggered the panic no longer matters. The problem becomes the actual sensations and the overwhelming fear of losing control.

Panic attacks can be overcome by: understanding panic, controlled belly breathing, changing the ANTs that are feeding the panic, and learning to cope with the *temporary* discomfort.

Panic can be driven by catastrophic thoughts—or panic can seem to have a life of its own and come out of nowhere. When the feeling starts, the individual automatically begins to think something like the following:

- "I will stop breathing."
- "I will faint."
- "I'm falling apart."
- "I will die."

For panic triggered by catastrophic thoughts, mastering the technique of belly breathing is critical. Relaxing is key to interrupting panic; in fact, relaxing is the opposite of catastrophizing. Focusing on your breath allows you to shift your thoughts away from unpleasant sensations. The slow, deep breaths will short-circuit the panic and return the body to its normal functioning.

If controlled breathing doesn't stop all the panic symptoms, the next step is to reassure yourself that the symptoms will subside, you will not faint, and you can get out of any situation in which you're feeling trapped. "I can handle a few minutes of this unpleasant feeling" is a good replacement thought for, "I am going crazy. I can't feel myself."

Panic often occurs when an individual finds him- or herself in a situation that seems to be a trap or to have no way out. An example is when you attend a party and suddenly feel hot, closed-in, or trapped with too many others. You might feel silly doing belly breaths in front of others, but no one will notice a few deep breaths, and you can always go to the restroom or outside for a few minutes. It also can be reassuring to just remind yourself that you can leave—the door is right there—or that the unpleasant feeling will pass. The cave dweller within you may just need a reminder that the situation is temporary, and, therefore, flight is unnecessary.

In combination with breathing and controlling your thoughts, it's important to go through the panic while remaining in the frightful situation. Our body believes the messages that we will die, faint, or perish if we stay in the room, drive over the bridge, or talk to that girl. However, the truth is that we will not meet a terrible fate if we stay put and maintain our focus. Instead, we will teach ourselves that the threatening situation is nothing of the sort. It is *not* threatening, just currently uncomfortable. We can manage the discomfort by breathing, getting on top of our ANTs, and giving ourselves a chance to have a new experience.

When panic attacks worsen, don't respond to your efforts to use these techniques, or get in the way of normal life, seek help from your doctor. Medications may be necessary in addition to learning these techniques, and only a professional can tell whether your form of panic requires further help. Because worry, fear, and panic are so uncomfortable and potentially debilitating, doing all you can to be free of their grip is worth it!

REST STOP

REMEMBERING
Key words and phrases: Can you define them?

The Worry Cycle _____

_____

Repetitive Checking Behavior _____

_____

Storyboarding _____

_____

Panic _____

_____

Test Anxiety _____

_____

Anticipatory Anxiety _____

_____

Relaxation _____

_____

Belly Breaths _____

_____

Flight Reflex _____

_____

Coping _____

_____

REFLECTING

Take time to ponder the following.

Do you like scary or violent television, movies, or video games? Why do you think so many people are fascinated by suspense and violence? Does the suspense or violence serve some kind of purpose? Is there anything detrimental about watching or reading these types of things? If you do not like scary or violent TV, movies, or video games, find others who enjoy the genres and ask them what they find appealing.

_____

_____

_____

_____

Ask one person in your family about what frightens them most in their daily lives. How do they get through their fears or manage their anxieties? What tools do they use to cope that could be helpful to you?

_____

_____

_____

_____

REINFORCING

Try these exercises to reinforce what you've learned.

1) Practice belly breathing every day in the morning and in the evening for three minutes.

2) Think of circumstances in which you normally feel anxious. Storyboard the experience to visualize succeeding or being comfortable in the situation.

3) This week when something comes up that you are anticipating anxiously, rehearse a positive outcome for the event. Do this aloud with someone you trust. Instruct him/her in being the "voice of worry." Coach him/her to voice all the things that could go wrong while you answer back with how you will handle things successfully.

4) For more insight and tips about the importance of reducing stress and anxiety, check out Goldie Hawn's 10 Mindful Minutes: Giving Our Children—and Ourselves—the Social and Emotional Skills to Reduce Stress and Anxiety for Healthier, Happy Lives.

RECORDING AND RESOLVING

Journal writing is a great tool for learning how to control your thoughts and feelings.

Record the ANTs you notice that lead to your anxiety. Then label and replace them with relaxing and realistic thoughts.

_____

_____

_____

_____

_____

_____

_____

_____

_____

_____

Remember:

EVENTS → INTERPRETATIONS → FEELINGS → ACTIONS

DEALING WITH DEPRESSION

Recently, depression is being discussed more and more. The media, middle school and high school health classes, popular fiction and music, and even parents and teachers are focusing on the subject.

Why, all of a sudden, is this topic so prevalent now? When your parents were your age, depression and its symptoms were "hidden away." The media's popular message at that time was that the majority of people were bubbly and happy with only minor and easy-to-solve problems. Think *Brady Bunch*.

In the recent past, mental health specialists didn't believe that teenagers *could* suffer from depression. The common belief was that "adolescents are just moody. It's all hormones." In the last decade, however, the epidemic of depression has become a matter of public concern. We've learned that depression is not some rare mental disorder that affects a few tortured souls but is much more widespread. In 2002, for example, the National Institute of Mental Health completed studies that found a significant increase in reported cases of depression, with nearly 3 million adolescents and as many as 15 million adults in the U.S. suffering from symptoms. That number of depressed teens equals about 11% of people between 11-18 years of age (National Institute of Mental Health Factsheet, 2014).

No one really knows if there are more cases of depression or if people are seeking help more freely. Some researchers speculate there are more adolescents suffering from this mood disorder because of changes in our social system—such as the stresses of divorced parents, increasing academic expectations, diminishing job possibilities, economic hardships, and increased pressure to be good-looking. Nonetheless, although the actual occurrence of depression is nothing new, what is new is the willingness for the public to address the problem.

Depression is a **mood disorder**, part of a group of psychiatric disorders characterized by a persistent disturbance of mood featuring low **self-esteem** and hopelessness. If someone has a healthy sense of self-esteem, or self-worth, he/she will have the confidence to forge ahead in the world. But you're not just born with self-esteem. According to the authors of *Face to Face: Cultivating Kids' Social Lives in Today's Digital World*, "self-esteem is the culmination of a process of [your] needs being met over time combined with the quality of [your] experiences as you grow" (Masarie, p. 6:13). Imagine if you grew up listening to the pesky ANTs of "should" statements (that you couldn't fulfill) or had positive attributes such as being "spirited" disqualified as being "difficult." Your self-esteem would be pretty low—and you'd be a good candidate for feeling hopeless and depressed.

Depression as a mood disorder is different from the **situational depression** everyone experiences at times in their lives due to events such as the death of a loved one, the discovery of a serious illness, divorce, or the breakup of a relationship. In these situations, the depression generally gets better as people reach out and offer their support, but problematic depression isn't cured by the attention, love, and encouragement of friends and family members nor by the passage of time. Instead, the feelings persist unless addressed by dealing with the ANTs that cause it, changing habits, and possibly taking medication.

In this chapter, you'll learn to identify the signs of depression in yourself and others as well as the ANTs that cause hopelessness. Depression is a serious issue you must take steps to address. We will direct you to resources that can help you beyond what this book can provide. We want to enable you to take actions that can transform hopelessness into creativity in your life.

THE SIGNS

How do you know if you or a loved one is suffering from depression? A pediatrician, psychiatrist, or licensed counselor would be the best suited to diagnose the issue, but you can look out for the symptoms, which include:

☐ Loss of appetite
☐ Flat mood
☐ Diminished interest in activities that once interested you
☐ Sleeping too much or too little
☐ Fatigue or a lack of energy
☐ Difficulty concentrating
☐ Difficulty making decisions
☐ Social withdrawal and isolation
☐ Suicidal thoughts and urges, or a plan for suicide
☐ Feelings of hopelessness, worthlessness, or excessive guilt
☐ Negative self-talk
☐ Low self-esteem
☐ Unresolved grief

WHAT DEPRESSION LOOKS LIKE

If it's helpful to think about what symptoms of depression may actually look like in your daily life, consider the following:

☐ Mild physical complaints such as headaches
☐ Frequent absences from school or withdrawing from activities
☐ A drop in grades
☐ Outbursts of anger, irritability, or frequent crying
☐ Sudden weight gain or weight loss
☐ Loss of interest in friends
☐ Dangerous or reckless behavior
☐ Overreacting to rejection, perceived judgment from others, or feelings of failure
☐ Harshly judging yourself and failing to see your good attributes

Do you recognize the symptoms in yourself or others in the descriptions of "What Depression Looks Like"? Do you wonder what caused these painful symptoms in the first place? Some researchers believe a variety of physiological factors negatively affect brain chemistry, resulting in the mood disorder. In this theory, depression is as naturally occurring as a kidney problem or impaired vision, so many doctors and counselors encourage their patients to use drugs called **anti-depressants**. For many people, these prescription drugs are an effective treatment and a huge relief.

But another theory is that depression is a thinking disorder caused and maintained by ANTs, and some patients find relief through controlling their ANTs. However, many still begin their recovery by taking medication. *An anti-depressant can lift that dark cloud high enough to see the clear path ahead.* Once on medication, you might have the energy to put into ANT control, which can enhance your mood and allow you to make additional inroads to feeling great.

It is critical to your well-being that you understand when it's necessary to reach out and get more help than this book can offer. **If you're struggling with thoughts of suicide or self-injury, if you are withdrawing from others, if you spend much of your time in despair, or if you feel that the pain has become too much, then it's time to ask for help.**

FEELING REALLY DEPRESSED?

Some ideas for where and how to get help are:

- If you're seriously thinking about hurting yourself, call 911 or go directly to the closest hospital emergency room.
- Talk to your parents, teachers, school counselors, or physician.
- Talk to your clergy, coach, school nurse, or any adult who has been a good listener to you in the past.
- Call your city's or county's crisis hotline. You can find this listed online or in the telephone yellow pages under "[Your city/county] Mental Health Crisis Hotline."
- Call your community mental health clinic. You can find this listed online or in the telephone yellow pages under "[Your city/community] Mental Health Clinic."

All 10 of the ANTs we explored earlier in this workbook can cause and maintain depression. Any one of the culprits could be leading the pack, but the ones that tend to underlie hopelessness, despair, and guilt are:

- All-or-nothing thinking
- Overgeneralization
- Mental filtering
- Labeling
- Catastrophizing

People feel hopeless about many things, both personal and global. In these seemingly dark times of war, terrorism, economic difficulty, and increased stresses and pressure, some individuals fall prey to the giant ANTs that lead them to believe that everything is dire and that things will never get better, only worse.

Hopelessness often is characterized by an inability to see beyond your view of the present moment. But, like all feelings, *hopelessness is always preceded by thoughts*. In personal hopelessness, you *forget* that you have had better times prior to your current state and that you will have better times again. In global, social, or political areas of hopelessness, you *fail to remember* that, just as there is pain in the world, there is also incredible goodness. Let's look more closely at these types of depressive thoughts.

Sydney first became depressed when she entered high school. Because of redistricting, Sydney didn't attend the same high school as her friends from middle school. She started out her freshman year without knowing many people, and, because she is shy, she had a difficult time making new friends. Although her parents encouraged her to try out for sports or join clubs, she felt paralyzed with self-consciousness and would not join any activities. Her freshman year was hard, even though she did make some casual friends with whom she was able to eat lunch and attend a few activities. Over the summer of her freshman year, she participated

in a soccer camp and did well. This gave her the confidence to successfully try out for the soccer team during her sophomore year. Sydney worked at soccer and gained respect from her teammates. This, in turn, made her feel better about her school, and she slowly improved her self-confidence enough to attend a few social activities. In her junior year, Sydney was also a stagehand for the musical and was doing well in her classes and making a few more friends.

In the middle of that year, however, Sydney's father lost his job. The worst part was that her father's best chance for employment was to move out of the area to the neighboring state and work with her uncle in his roofing business. Sadly, in the middle of her junior year, Sydney had to move to a new town, a new high school, and a new group of people she was certain wouldn't welcome her.

At first, Sydney suffered sadness caused by the uprooting change, just as most people would. But what may have begun as a situational depression deepened and continued throughout the year, the summer, and into her senior year. Sydney's hopelessness had taken hold with devastating consequences. No matter how much her mom tried to cheer her, involve her, and remind her that she had built friendships before and could do it again, Sydney could not get herself to feel differently about her new situation.

Sydney was plagued by thoughts of hopelessness. On a daily basis, she told herself, "I'll never have friends here. Everyone already has their friends, and they don't want more. I'm so unlucky. Everything is always so hard in my life. My life is 10 times worse than these people's. They have all had one another for years. They won't want me on their soccer team. I'm not even going to try out. I'll never be comfortable here. I can't even figure out why I'm alive. My life is ruined. I was just getting popular, and now I am the only person here without someone. I am such a loser! Who would want to get to know me? I hate this school anyway. Why didn't I just stay there on my own? I hate my dad for moving us here. It's so stupid." And her negative thoughts went on and on.

Sydney's ANTs became so bad that her grades were falling, her desire to attend a state college was in jeopardy, and, with the exception of school, she hardly left the house. Although Sydney had joined soccer in her senior year, she was so tired from not sleeping, so self-critical and numb, that her ability to handle the ball was diminished. The worse she played, the worse she felt, and that continued the negative downward spiral. This depressed girl was driving herself into the ground.

Let's look at some of Sydney's thinking errors:

"I'll never have friends here. Everyone already has their friends, and they don't want more." This is an example of mind reading and negatively predicting the future. The truth is, making good friends in a new school can be difficult, but we cannot predict with certainty what will happen if we try. As challenging as it is to overcome shyness, Sydney may have made friends if she could have given 100% to the soccer team. She may have made friends if she had smiled, spoken up, asked people if she could join them at the table, worked on the school plays, joined a service organization, or attended a youth group at the church her family attended.

"I'm so unlucky. Everything is always so hard in my life. My life is 10 times worse than these people." Here's an unfortunate example of all-or-nothing thinking, labeling, mental filtering, disqualifying the positive, and mind reading! Yikes! Sydney has covered all the bases to assure some miserable feelings. Realistically thinking, everything is not always hard. That is classic all-or-nothing thinking. Moving can be very difficult, but negative thinking makes it all worse. Sydney is catastrophizing when she assumes that she has a worse life than most people. In fact, her life is better than some, worse than some, and better at some times than at other times.

"They won't want me on their soccer team. I'm not even going to try out. I'll never be comfortable here." Here, Sydney is jumping to conclusions, and the conclusions aren't pretty!

"I can't even figure out why I'm alive. My life is ruined." Sydney is catastrophizing when she thinks her life is ruined. Sydney is 17 years old with her whole life ahead of her. It might be a tough year ahead, and, then again, it might not. But, bottom line, a year from now she will have moved on to college and will be starting out again with people from all over. Whenever we think that the way things are today dictates how they will be tomorrow, we are jumping to conclusions.

Sydney is also mental filtering. She can only see the negative aspects of life and cannot incorporate the good things into her view. For Sydney, life is completely dark. Never mind that she now lives in another nice home, her health is excellent, and her friends from the past stay in contact with her—yay, technology! This example of mental filtering is one with potentially devastating consequences. When Sydney is wondering why she should bother, she is standing on a slippery slope that can end in self-harm.

"I am such a loser! Who would want to get to know me?" This is labeling. Remember, this is a thinking error because you're dwelling on your flaws or perceived flaws rather than seeing yourself as a person with both strengths and weaknesses. In a non-depressed state, Sydney might see she is shy and acknowledge she needs to put in extra effort to get to know people who had established their friendships years before. In labeling and in personalizing, we highlight our flaws, rather than practicing a balanced view that leads to more self-acceptance.

Poor Sydney. She is cycling deeper and deeper into despair. We don't want to leave her there, so we're going to send her to the new family physician who notices that Sydney has many of the symptoms of depression and suggests she work with a wonderful social worker in town who treats adolescents.

With her therapist, Sydney learned all about ANTs and began to keep a journal to work on her daily moods. With her therapist, Sydney decided that, if therapy didn't help enough within three months, she would get an evaluation for anti-depressants. In three months, however, Sydney was doing great! She was involved with the drama department on the stage crew, was dating a guy from her Economics class, and was pulling up her grades. She had managed to regain her concentration and do well enough on her SATs to get accepted into several colleges!

TREATING DEPRESSION

Untreated depression is the cause of some very serious consequences. The biggest concern is that of suicide or self-injury. Sadly, *suicide is the third leading cause of death among 10- to 24-year-olds.* Self-injury can take such forms as cutting or burning oneself; high-risk behavior involving drugs, alcohol, or sexual experimentation; and general poor self-care in which an individual simply does not make good choices for him- or herself.

Hopelessness leads to despair, and it is all too easy for the despair to lead to an impulsive act. Depression and hopelessness can always be treated; in fact, treatment for depression is one of the most successful treatments the medical community can offer. As noted earlier, depression is a mood disorder, and moods change. That's why we call them moods! The problem lies in believing that the pain is permanent or, even worse, that the pain is part of your real personality.

Remembering that you only want the pain to stop—that you really do not want to stop being alive—is the first step toward getting the help you need. Pain can be ended without ending your life. If you broke your leg and were in incredible pain, the

INTERESTING FACT

Suicide is not a solution; it is a permanent response to a temporary problem.

emergency room doctor would not kill you. She would give you medicine and fix your leg. One should not die over emotional pain either. There is help, usually only a phone call or a doctor's visit away.

If you are thinking about suicide, are seriously planning a suicide attempt, or think something inside of you is pressuring you to end your life, you must seek help now.

The same goes if someone you know is in the same situation; help that friend get help. Please tell someone right away. You can tell your parent, your minister, the police, your teacher, or any responsible adult; go to an emergency room; or call 911. Please take this action now. You're worth it! Your friend is worth it!

"We are at the very beginning of time for the human race. It is not unreasonable that we grapple with problems. But there are tens of thousands of years in the future. Our responsibility is to do what we can, learn what we can, improve the solutions, and pass them on."

– Richard Feynman

HOW TO FIND THE POSITIVE IN TROUBLING TIMES

For many people, the main source of their feelings of hopelessness stems from political, social, and environmental concerns. Some overwhelmingly believe the world's problems have never been as dangerous, gloomy, and doomed as they are today. Is this a fact, or is this a collection of thinking errors fed in part by our limited understanding of the facts and by the spotlight of the media?

Every day unnecessary suffering takes place in our world. Wars, school shootings, suicide bombers, unemployment, disease, famine, and environmental disasters . . . you name it, it happens. Why do we know when bad stuff happens? Because we have a widespread network of media. We have access to news 24/7, and, if we tune out for a bit, someone at school or work will quickly bring us up to date by asking, "Did you hear the news?" Because of the influence of the media, all of us are aware of the frightening things going on, and there seem to be so many.

INTERESTING FACT

There are people working hard on solutions for all of the problems that cause us pain.

The media focuses on the stories that will catch our attention, which tend to be suspenseful, scary, glamorous, or sensational. If we're walking through a room with the television on and hear a reporter say, "There was a school shooting today in Kentucky," we'll be more likely to stop and pay attention than if we hear news that says, "Today in Kentucky ten teenagers raised $5,000 for charity." Humans love drama, pure and simple.

"But wait," you say, "things *are* grim in the world." You're right; life can be harsh. The trouble is, however, that the frightening stuff gets the headlines while the attempts at the solutions go underreported. All problems have some people working hard on solving them. As a group, we mentally filter and catastrophize to a point where most of us believe everything is getting worse and that life is hopeless now, for certain.

In fact, not everything is getting worse. It's all in what you focus on, where you get your information, and how hard you try to look beyond the simple headlines. In 2001, for example, statistics noted that violent crime in America was down by 25%, while at the same time the *reporting* of violent crime was up by 300%. Go figure! While the media focuses on school shootings (which are horrible but not daily occurrences) and America becomes frightened and concerned about how violent teenagers are becoming, an in-depth survey found that today's generation of adolescents give more time to charity than any previous generation. Teenagers who work at the blood drive, feed the homeless, tutor, or clean up the beach are just not exciting enough to make the headlines. In truth, many, many more altruistic events take place than scary ones.

- In one Western city, high school girls organized to collect used prom dresses to redistribute at other schools so that girls who couldn't afford formalwear could choose from a closet full of dresses that have never been worn at their school.

- In a Midwestern city, a high school boy began collecting blankets for the homeless and goes out at night after dark in the cold distributing them to those who live on his city's streets.

- Recently, a group of girls shaved their heads to lend support to their friend who was losing her hair from the side effects of chemotherapy.

Joining in, on whatever level is possible for you, to become part of the solution is one of the greatest antidotes for depression. Many successful therapists have treated depression

> For each horror story, there is a story out there of someone working hard to bring peace and harmony to that very injustice.

by insisting that the client only return to therapy once he or she had started volunteering in the community. What these creative therapists saw in their most depressed clients was that, once they focused on helping somebody else, their thoughts automatically became more hopeful. It makes good sense.

ACTIONS THAT LEAD TO CREATING A NEW REALITY

Look, let's face it: We are all in this world together and others' actions, moods, and vibes are supposed to affect us on some level. We know, we know, we have been lecturing you for chapters that our thoughts create our moods, and that how we view the world is the real problem. Okay, that is still true, but part of the real solution lies in how we all come to the day. If we come to the day with thoughts of hopelessness, or, if we come to the day with a "who cares" attitude, then we become part of the problems making everyone feel hopeless!

In actuality, people who suffer from depression are often those with the biggest hearts. These individuals aren't actually glum and negative about themselves by nature. More often, depressed people are the ones who see the aches and pains of their families, friends, and even the world. They cannot walk past the

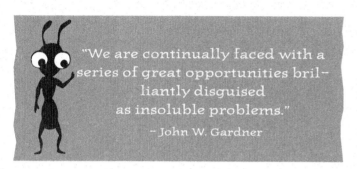

"We are continually faced with a series of great opportunities brilliantly disguised as insoluble problems."

– John W. Gardner

park bench where an elderly woman sits alone and not feel upset. Instead, depressed individuals are often prone to noticing those scenarios, embellishing them a bit with thinking errors, and feeling helpless to have any impact. It is the **helplessness** we wish to challenge.

Helplessness and hopelessness are best friends joined hand-in-hand at all times. They eat, drink, sleep, and attend functions as one. *To truly combat the ANTs of hopelessness, you will need to confront helpless thoughts with hopeful actions.*

We are far from helpless beings. We have, in fact, been changing things since we arrived on the planet. Remember our cave-dwelling friend? Although he is a part of each of us, for the most part we have adapted way beyond him.

The actions, activities, and thoughts of *hope* are largely responsible for these changes, both the subtle ones and the major accomplishments of humankind. What are these hope-based thoughts and actions? They consist of the smallest of things which, when consistently applied, bring the biggest of changes. These are inner human resources, such as the ability to:

AS HUMANS,
WE HAVE THE INNER RESOURCES TO:

	Pray	Ask
	Persist	Laugh
Prepare	Smile	Be Patient
Care	Focus	Share
Believe	Act	Imagine
Forgive	Trust	Be Confident
Change	Accept	Contribute
Risk	Wait	Dream
Listen	Connect	Rest
Relax	Understand	Invent

In addition to challenging and replacing the ANTs of hopelessness, changing the way we come to the day gives us the capacity to create the kind of life about which we feel good. In fact, coming to the day with hope helps us to live life "on purpose."

We are all inherently resourceful. Hope makes us resilient enough to face our adversity by looking at our resources and deciding which options might help in a particular situation. In fact, resilient people see the problems before them as challenges they are ready and able to face.

REST STOP

REMEMBERING
Key words and phrases: Can you define them?

Mood Disorder _____

_____

Self-Esteem _____

_____

Anti-Depressant _____

_____

Hopelessness _____

_____

Mental Filter _____

_____

Helplessness _____

_____

Catastrophize _____

_____

Situational Depression _____

_____

REFLECTING
Take time to ponder the following.

After reading over the list of symptoms of depression in this chapter, do you think you're depressed? If yes, how low are you feeling? Is it time to seek the help of an adult?

If you need(ed) help with depression, who are the adults to
whom you could turn? Why would each person be a good choice?

_____

_____

_____

_____

_____

How much time are you spending doing community service?
Can you do more? Are there opportunities you might explore to
tackle some of the problems in your community? Volunteering
at a cat shelter? Serving meals to the homeless? Pulling invasive
species of plants? You get the idea.

_____

_____

_____

_____

REINFORCING
Try these exercises to reinforce what you've learned.

1) Copy the hopeful words at the end of this chapter onto
brightly colored paper and cut them out. Along with pictures of
hope you find in magazines, cover the borders of an inexpensive
picture frame with these words. Put a picture of yourself in the
frame and place it in a prominent location in your room. Each
time you see yourself framed by these hopeful messages, remember you are building a framework through which you view the
world and your own life.

2) Ask family members and friends who have experienced difficult times how they remain hopeful. Ask people whom you admire how they "frame" their life stories.

RECORDING AND RESOLVING

Journal writing is a great tool for learning how to control your thoughts and feelings.

Keep a journal for two days of any and all hopeless thoughts you find yourself thinking. As with all negative thoughts, label them and replace them with balanced thinking and resilient approaches. Try to notice what preceded the thoughts. Are your hopeless thoughts fed by movies, songs, news websites, or evening news?

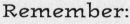

Remember:

EVENTS → INTERPRETATIONS → FEELINGS → ACTIONS

UNDERSTANDING RELATIONSHIPS

Probably the most important thing in life is relationships—with your friends, family, boyfriend, girlfriend, partner, mentors, teachers. . . . The reason nothing else is as important goes back to our caveman friend.

Early people lived in the open, vulnerable to predators and other humans. They didn't have big teeth and claws to defend themselves. Instead, for protection, nothing was more important than "belonging." If accepted by his fellow tribesmen, a caveman would be protected by the entire tribe because each early human's brain was wired for attachment to others of the same species; this "attachment" prompted cavemen to watch out for each other.

Although we don't depend upon each other in the same ways as our ancestors did, we still carry similar needs. We all crave to feel connected, included, and protected. "Belonging" is so important that our brain is wired to make us feel strong attractions to others. Sometimes, that attraction even tricks us into seeing some people as "perfect." (More on that later.)

> ### INTERESTING FACT
>
> **We are born into relationships, we are shaped by relationships, and we are looking for someone who fits into the shapes.**

Our first relationships form us the most. From birth until about six years of age, our brain is continually recording human relating. How we are treated directly and what we see happen between people **imprints** upon us what to expect from close relationships. Some of the imprint can be terrific, and some of it can be painful.

All the positive and negative experiences of childhood are recorded or imprinted in your brain. Yours is a unique imprint, because no one in the world had your same childhood experiences. This imprint colors how you will behave in your relationships. It even dictates what romantic love will look and feel like to you. Because of its deep complexity, it's romantic love we will focus on in this chapter.

UNDERSTANDING YOUR LOVE MAP

When you reach the age of seeking intimacy, your imprinted "Love Map" will surface, leading you to know what type of person looks "right" to you and how love "should" feel. Some relationship experts put it this way: We are born into relationships, we are shaped by relationships, and we are looking for someone who fits into the shapes.

It's all about attraction! Attraction is an exciting experience. Someone piques your interest. Someone seems "just right." You may think that cute person across the room makes your heart skip a beat. But your brain is really skipping a beat and talking to the neurons around your heart.

In essence, exciting as attraction is, it's just a chemical reaction! Meeting a particular someone triggers a release of chemicals in your brain to let you know that the person has some important qualities—*qualities reminiscent of the memories you recorded when you were little*! This is called **familiar love**.

SOMETHING ABOUT THIS PERSON IS FAMILIAR

Your brain recognizes when someone seems familiar to you—not familiar as in, "Didn't I meet you at a party last week?" Rather, familiar in an unconscious way. Perhaps the person's personality just "feels right." Maybe the person seems easy to talk to or immediately "gets you."

What's happening in this situation is that your brain is bringing up your old imprints and notices how this new person is a "match" of someone from your past experiences. This mental process then ignites the chemical spark of attraction. All this goes on in a part of your brain of which you have little awareness. At the time, you don't realize the person reminds you of your mom, dad, babysitter, grandparent, or sibling. In fact, the person is a teenager, so why would he or she be anything like either of your parents or any of your caregivers?

Besides being familiar in good ways, a person you find attractive might also be a "match" because his or her negative qualities match the negative experiences you had with your parents and/or others. Your conscious mind doesn't register this. In fact, when you're attracted to someone, you don't see his or her negative traits. You *minimize* his or her flaws. In fact, your brain hides the negative qualities from you, so you focus only on the good traits. This feature of your Love Map can be of concern because, if you were neglected or abused in your past, then the traits of neglect and abuse are wired into your brain as part of your picture of love. This wiring could lead to your tolerating poor treatment by a partner.

Your Love Map is also designed to lead you to a person who has qualities that will challenge you. For example, you might think: "He rejects my opinions, just like my brother," or "She doesn't follow through on promises, just like my mom."

OPPOSITES ATTRACT . . .
AND THEN WE DRIVE EACH OTHER CRAZY

But your brain is curious about difference. So your Love Map might also lead you to people who are different from you in some fundamental ways. Because the brain is tricky, and romance is one of its famous tricks, you, at first, will think the person is the same as you. Maybe because our cave ancestors were afraid of difference and at the same time needed new blood in the tribe, the brain has to trick us into not seeing the differences at first.

Humans are attracted to difference because it helps us grow, completes us, challenges us, and exposes a part of us that we haven't yet developed. Maybe you're very in touch with your feelings and are a deep thinker but you aren't physically active nor drawn to get out and use your many senses in the world. Your brain will try to match you with someone who loves physical activity but isn't that much into reading. Sound ridiculous and illogical? It does to us, too. But scientists and relationship counselors have been noting this phenomenon for decades. Through their research, we have learned that one of the purposes of attraction is to help you to grow, accept parts of yourself, and change parts of yourself.

If you really like someone, for example, you will stretch out of your comfort zone to try new things. Mostly that is a good thing, but sometimes a person who is attracted to someone and very overtaken by the "romance chemicals" will join in activities that go against deep beliefs. This is one reason bullies have a following—because people are only seeing the good traits in someone they find attractive and want so badly to be liked in return. It isn't hard to understand why good people sometimes ignore very bad behavior.

THE UPS AND DOWNS OF RELATIONSHIPS

All relationships, romances as well as friendships, go through predictable stages. Knowing this could help you to have more peace. In the fluid relationships of your teen years, you will most likely have one or two connections that last and many temporary ones that fit your current needs but eventually end. In other words, there will be many ups and downs, and relationships will come and go. When you stay long term in an adult, committed relationship, there are more stages than just ups and downs. Marriages work when a couple learns tools that help them to overcome conflict and stay committed to a stable, loving partnership.

THE "UP" STAGE: ATTRACTION/ATTACHMENT

The first stage of relationships is the time of attraction and attachment to a new person. If it's a romantic interest, then a "crush" forms. Even if it's just friendship, the relationship still may have a high energy feel to it.

The brain chemistry of having a crush on someone or having a new best friend is very intense. During this attachment stage, brain chemicals trigger wonderful feelings about the new person. The hormones released cause you to feel energetic, focused, positive, a little obsessive, and as though you have known this person your whole life. Remember, though, that the person seems familiar because he or she is like your family or a caregiver in many ways; he or she "fits" your Love Map.

During the attraction/attachment stage of a relationship, many thinking errors occur. Whereas the process of falling in love equates to automatic positive thoughts, you have on blinders and can't fully see. You might minimize flaws, label your partner as perfect, jump to the conclusion you will live happily ever after, and blame everyone else for his or her bad behavior—or your own bad behavior.

The attraction/attachment stage is also called **infatuation** and is designed to bond you to one another. This happens because the chemicals of attraction make you feel terrific when you're with your love interest, and terrible when you are not. As a result, you suddenly like yourself and your life so much better!

The romance chemicals also increase your willingness to take risks. You will try things that haven't interested you in the past. Maybe you are normally shy and your attraction makes you open and outspoken. The risks also can be dangerous. Attraction chemicals can make you drink, use drugs, drive fast, break the law, and stop being truthful to your parents and friends. In addition, they can make you aggressive and jealous. This can lead to attempts to retaliate against your boyfriend or girlfriend or anyone you see as threatening to your relationship.

In the attraction/attachment stage of relationships, sexual desire increases. We can look back to our caveman ancestor for understanding why. In addition to fulfilling our need to belong to the tribe, the chemicals of attraction/attachment also fulfill our biological drive to meet, mate, and procreate. In ancient times, humans needed to have a compelling reason to bond and connect with one another; there was a lot of physical adversity then, so our sex drive needed to be strong enough to overcome all the obstacles to pair bonding that life on the savannah created!

Fast forward thousands of years. Today, the sex drive is still strong and immediate. Even if you think of sex as just "hooking-up," sex is actually designed to make you feel attached to a partner and possibly attached to the outcome of the interaction: a relationship and a baby.

THE "DOWN" STAGE: WHERE DID THE CHEMISTRY GO?

Eventually everything that goes up comes down. This is also true with the chemistry of romantic feelings. They aren't designed to last forever. On average, romantic feelings come on very quickly and last a few weeks to a year.

When the brain chemicals wear off or change, you can feel as "down" as you once felt "up." That isn't because your love interest was the wrong person for you, but, rather, because enough time passed that your brain decided you had bonded as a pair and no longer needed the extra chemicals on board. Remember this biochemistry has been going on a long time throughout human history, and romantic love's purpose is to connect you with another person. Once you are with a partner, you don't need infatuation. In the time of our ancestors, you would have conceived a child and settled down to ensure that child's survival.

The passing of the infatuation stage is a sad reality and brings up many painful moments including **power struggles**. When a power struggle occurs, bad behaviors can surface. For example, perhaps you used to stay up all night talking or texting. Now that the romance is breaking down, you may stay up arguing or breaking up.

The brain chemistry of a power struggle can leave you feeling despair, deep grief, blind rage, and hopeless. It can even lead you to think you are worthless and maybe life isn't worth living. You may think your pain stems from missing the person on whom you had a crush. Instead, the real truth is that you miss how great you felt when you were infatuated with that special someone.

Power struggles really trigger ANT invasions! You may personalize the change in the mood and behaviors of your boy- or girlfriend. Instead of looking at how you have changed, you just notice how poorly you are being treated and judge the treatment as unfair.

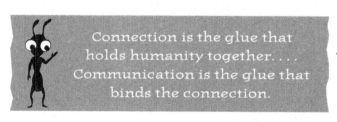

Connection is the glue that holds humanity together. . . . Communication is the glue that binds the connection.

You then blame your partner, and, if the relationship gets rocky or ends, you may have many moments of thinking what you "should" have done differently. If you go on angry long enough, you will begin to name call, diss your ex, and label yourself, him, or her as a jerk or loser.

Other common ANTs during power struggles are mind reading and jumping to jealous conclusions. If a boyfriend or girlfriend is no longer being nice, it must be that "he or she is cheating or starting up with someone new." This type of thinking only makes matters worse. It leads to more fights, crying, and misunderstanding.

Last of all, you may mental filter, view your whole life as terrible, and, ultimately, feel full of hopelessness and despair. This pain can be intolerable at times and trigger an impulse to hurt yourself, make you distracted at school and sports, and/or cause anxiety and depression.

WHAT MAKES RELATIONSHIPS WORK?

Despite knowing that relationships can fall apart, humans rarely give up trying to connect with others. That's because, along with food and shelter, relationships are necessary for survival. In fact, connection is the glue that holds humanity together. But, without infatuation chemicals, stable connection is hard to maintain. Even mature adults who can hold down jobs and be good parents can end up getting a divorce. What does ensure lasting and enjoyable relationships is consistent nurturing and hard work on the part of both partners—work that includes heartfelt commitment and good, clear communication.

At different stages of your life, commitment means different things. There's a lifelong commitment to family that most of us maintain. That kind of commitment is characterized by a sense of loyalty and a love without condition.

But commitment to those outside the family usually doesn't come as easily, and, in your adolescent years, commitment isn't even a huge priority. Sure, you are drawn to people and plan to know them forever, but your brain is wired to bounce back fairly well when you end a relationship. That is, as much as it can be agonizing to break off a close relationship, your brain knows you have much more time to find someone with whom you will sustain a commitment. In fact, for teens, commitment is often much about honesty and following through on your word.

The twin of "commitment" in relationships is "communication." The dictionary defines *communication* as "the exchange of thoughts, messages, or information, as by speech, signals, writing, or behavior." In other words, communication isn't just what you say aloud.

If connection is the glue that holds together humanity, then communication is the glue that binds the connection. And, just like connection is hard to maintain, communicating accurately and successfully is challenging. In fact, one researcher has found over and over that "people don't correctly

understand even half of what they hear" (Gottman). That's because our brains are wired to decode lots of information from various sources, and sometimes the decoding is accurate and sometimes it's not. Sometimes our communication comprises misunderstandings and automatic negative thoughts. Sometimes people are in their own heads so much they don't hear the true messages from their special person.

The culprits of miscommunication include our lack of paying attention, our mental filtering and jumping to conclusions, and our defensiveness when someone is communicating their upsets. All these reactions are completely normal and how our brain naturally reacts when confronted with the stress of any threat to connection.

Some misunderstandings occur because communicating is our attempt to share information about our needs, desires, perceptions, and feelings, and, yet, most of us don't know how to accurately describe our real feelings or to say what we need without complaining. Mastering the art of communication takes work and maturity. Having good communication role models makes learning how to communicate easier, but it's harder if you have poor modeling at home.

WHAT CAN YOU DO
TO BECOME A GOOD COMMUNICATOR?

Are you interested in improving your communication skills so you better connect with the person you're dating? Do you want to fight less and live more harmoniously with your parents? Do you want to talk to your friends without drama?

One major tip we want to share that will help you be successful at the communication part of relationships is to remember that everyone has a unique and valuable point of view and that everyone's point of view is just as valuable as your own. One communication expert, Dr. Harville Hendrix, suggests we live from the mindset that "everyone's opinion and point of view is as valid as my own." Wow! Can you imagine the reduction in conflict if that were the way we all operated?

Below are some tips that come from the two relationship experts we mentioned above, Dr. Gottman and Dr. Hendrix. Note: Texting is not a good form of communication other than for the purpose of giving information. Rather, communication requires eliminating distractions, taking turns, and being clear about your intentions.

Successful Listening Rules

1. *Always try to understand the situation from the other's point of view.* What a challenge! Understanding a parent's point of view may require listening to and acknowledging a lot of fears you don't share. With your peers, you may be "trying on" various opinions and viewpoints, and they may be "trying on" opinions and viewpoints with you; the viewpoint(s) can change daily or even hourly! With a romantic interest, you might struggle with listening to his or her disappointment in your behavior. Whatever the situation, imagine you are crossing a bridge over to the other person's world, opening up to understanding what it is like to be in his or her shoes.

2. *Listen without interrupting, showing contempt, or being defensive. Good listeners make it safe for the other to speak.* If reactions arise, take a deep breath and cancel any annoying defensive thoughts so you can focus on listening. Showing contempt includes sighing, rolling your eyes, or saying anything sarcastic.

3. *Never ridicule the speaker's point of view.* You need to show respect for another's opinions by stretching yourself to wait until the end of the speaker's turn and then actually validating the speaker. Validation is the verbal demonstration that we understand where the speaker is coming from and it makes sense to us. Agreement isn't the goal nor is it even important. Just say, "You make sense to me." What if what the person says doesn't make sense to you? The theory we hold about listening is that, if you successfully put aside the need to be right, if you are curious about the other's opinion, and if you remember you aren't looking for agreement, what the person says will make sense. It will make sense because you can see and hear the real person and their message.

4. *Now imagine what it is like to stand in his or her shoes.* When you imagine what the speaker feels about what he or she shared, this is called **empathy.** It is a form of feeling with the speaker instead of being off in your own world. When

you think of what the other person might feel, ask if you are guessing correctly. This is important! You might imagine that the speaker is angry with you, and it's not about you at all. This gives him or her a chance to correct your conclusion or confirm it.

5. *If you have a response, wait a few moments and then ask the speaker if he or she would be willing to hear what you have to say.* Always take a deep breath and imagine walking back over that bridge to your own world and seeing what your point of view is *after listening.* Your particular viewpoint may be the same, stronger, or completely different after considering the other person's point of view.

Talking So Others Can Listen

1. *Before you ask to talk about something difficult, know what you want from the conversation.* Do you just want to be listened to without advice? Maybe you are asking for support or help. Maybe you want a shoulder to cry on. All these are good intentions. Knowing what you are hoping for will make for a better outcome. Approach your friend, parent, or partner by being clear about what you need. For example, you might say, "Mom, I need to talk about something important, but I just need you to listen and not give advice. Okay?" Or, "I just need you to listen, because I want you to understand what I'm really trying to say. When I'm done, I will listen to you."

2. *Don't attack the listener.* Avoid "you" statements such as, "You didn't call me yesterday and I waited around all day." "You" statements are blaming, and filled with "should" and "shouldn'ts." Instead, use "I" statements such as, "Yesterday, when I didn't hear back from you, I felt hurt. If you can't call me, please just send a text and let me know you aren't available." Most people don't really mean to hurt others, so assume there has been a misunderstanding and there is no need for blame. Blame never solves problems.

3. *Ask for what you need versus complaining or whining.* This is super hard. We bet your parents don't even do this very well. Complaining is a "need in disguise." A big opportunity in adolescence is to learn what

it is you need and find people to whom you can honestly express your needs.

4. *Get to the point.* Don't repeat yourself over and over. You may like hearing the sound of your voice and it might feel great to have attention, but don't wear out the listener. It can cause him or her to be impatient with you.

5. *Pick a good time to talk.* Late at night, on the phone, or through texting might not be appropriate for working through problems. For example, don't break up on the phone or via text, unless you think that the person you are ending things with is dangerous. Otherwise, ask to get together to talk. This goes for friendships, too. If you feel hurt or slighted by a friend, ask to sit down and talk face-to-face.

6. *Speak directly to the person with whom you are upset.* Don't go to others and vent about someone. It's disrespectful, hurtful, and increases the drama. No one likes to be talked about behind his or her back.

FINAL THOUGHTS ABOUT RELATIONSHIPS

Relationships are the most important thing in most people's lives. They are also the most challenging. They take work, whether they are with a romantic partner, friends, or family.

What you can do about the normal challenges of relationships is to listen to the stories you tell yourself about other people. Are you mind reading, jumping to conclusions, taking their behavior personally, or blaming them for problems? Until you free your own thinking of ANTs, you can't do a decent job of communicating what you feel and need. So, take a look at your negative thinking spiral and straighten it out. Then talk to your partner, parent, or friend.

Final words of wisdom: Be generous to those you like and love, and we aren't talking about giving gifts. Be generous with your patience, your honesty (not the stinging kind), your forgiveness, and your understanding. All these actions will go a long way toward prolonging connection and strengthening your relationships—making your life more rewarding, peaceful, and fun.

REST STOP

REMEMBERING
Key words and phrases: Can you define them?

Imprints _____

_____

Familiar Love _____

_____

Infatuation _____

_____

Love Map _____

_____

Empathy _____

_____

REFLECTING
Take time to ponder the following.

During this month, pay close attention to your thoughts about
people you are getting to know and really like, and those you
have known for a while and with whom you have a few issues.
Do you put new crushes on a pedestal? Do you find fault with
your existing friends? Considering what you've learned in this
chapter, why do you think this happens?

_____

_____

_____

_____

Ask yourself how you behave in relationships at your best and at your worst. What traits and behaviors would you like to improve?

_____

_____

_____

_____

REINFORCING

Try these exercises to reinforce what you've learned.

1) When you next have an issue with a friend or partner, try the communication tips we suggested. What worked? What didn't work?

_____

_____

_____

_____

2) The next time you're upset with your parent(s), ask him/her/them to read the communication tips. Then sit down and have a conversation about the tools, role play some scenarios using the tools, and see if you all can commit to trying out the tools during future conflicts. Did some of the tools resonate more with you and your parent(s) than others? Which one(s) would you like to make a part of your life?

_____

_____

_____

_____

RECORDING AND RESOLVING

Journal writing is a great tool for learning how to control your thoughts and feelings.

1. Draw a big circle and divide the circle in half horizontally.
2. On the top half, write all (at least 10; generate as many as you can) of the positive traits of your parent(s): e.g., funny, generous, stable, spiritual, clever, hardworking, etc.
3. On the bottom half, write all (at least 10; generate as many as you can) of the negative traits of your parent(s): e.g., mean, unfriendly, strict, over working, alcoholic, depressed, sad, selfish, etc.
4. Next, underline the 5 best traits of your parent(s) and the 5 worst traits.
5. Then write these best and worst traits in list form.
6. Now think of your strongest love interests or best friends. Write their names next to the traits on the list and begin to see if your Love Map becomes clear.

Do you see any pattern of familiar love? How are your closest peers similar to and different from your family? Do you see the positive and negative traits of your parent(s) in your personality? Take time to journal about what you think and how you feel about your emerging Love Map.

Remember:

EVENTS → INTERPRETATIONS → FEELINGS → ACTIONS

PRACTICING COMPASSION

In a book about thinking errors, why are we bringing up a topic that sounds religious or spiritual? Because this is a workbook about "owning" your mind so you live your best life—and compassion is, first, a matter of the mind and, second, a matter of how to live.

The human brain is unique in the amount of brain area devoted to compassion. Remember the prefrontal cortex area we named "Consciousness Central"? This part of the brain is larger and more developed than the other parts of the brain in humans. It is responsible for generating thoughts of understanding, compassion, and empathy. Because we think those thoughts, our bodies feel the emotions of tenderness, sadness, sympathy, love, spiritual connection, and peace. (It must come as no surprise that dogs also have a well-developed prefrontal cortex! Most of us recognize in dogs an ability to comfort us, accept us, and instantly forgive us if we step on their tails or snap at them.)

In general, the brain activity of the prefrontal cortex moves us to understand others as well as ourselves. When we think we are safe (a function of the reptil-

> "Exchange judgment for curiosity, and being right, for being kind.
> – Virginia Satir

ian brain), we can be curious about others and what it's like to stand in their shoes. The prefrontal cortex also helps us to grasp that others are different from us and that it is okay they are different. Our reptilian brain recognizes difference but views difference as dangerous. If the part of the brain that sees danger is a "lizard with radar" watching out for our safety, this part of our brain is a "monk" striving for understanding and wisdom.

The need to be in touch with the understanding and compassionate part of our nature is perhaps more important now than at any other time in human history. Increased migration of the planet's people has made nearly every nation a more diverse place to live. Living from a viewpoint that difference is interesting, not dangerous, gives us the capacity to live side-by-side peacefully, sharing our planet's resources. In other chapters when we have discussed ANTs, we haven't suggested that you adopt a viewpoint different from your automatic negative thoughts. Rather, we taught you to challenge your flawed thinking, change the thoughts, and get on with your day. In our discussion of compassion, we hope to inspire you to change the basis of how you view everyone in the world. We hope you will see the benefits of a life lived from the viewpoint that all of us are worthy of understanding, acceptance, and concern. We hope you will begin to see that, whereas others may think and behave differently from you, we all have equally valid thoughts and feelings.

So, what exactly is compassion, where does it come from, and how do we cultivate a **compassionate viewpoint**?

COMPASSION IS:

- Patience
- Walking in another's shoes
- Empathy
- Curiosity
- Accepting our own and others' limitations
- Recognizing others as different but equal
- Sympathetic consciousness of another's distress together with a desire to alleviate the pain or problem
- Putting unconditional love into action
- Coming from the heart
- Forgiveness
- Recognizing that we have some of the same flaws for which we judge others

COMPASSION IS NOT:

- Pity
- Condoning behavior that you believe is not moral, healthy, or acceptable
- Denial of harmful, hurtful, addictive, or unhealthy behaviors
- Enabling of any of the above
- Doing for others what they will not do for themselves
- Being a pushover
- Caretaking or saving others
- Ignoring our differences

Some people are confused about what compassion really means. They may identify it as a "weak" emotion, when, in fact, it takes great strength to put into practice.

In its most basic form, to be compassionate is to be curious and understanding. It also involves realizing we don't need to find fault with nor fear others. Instead, when we practice compassion, we endeavor to understand others in the context of their reality. Think how a monk might think.

Just like all feelings, you can only *feel* compassion toward yourself or others when you *think* compassionate thoughts. Infants and preschool children are thought to have automatic compassion responses to distressed people and animals. Over time, some of those automatic reactions are socialized out of us by hearing prejudiced and fear-based messages at home and in school. Most adolescents and adults need to cultivate compassion in order to have a mature viewpoint of understanding and respecting others.

Think about our favorite formula:

EVENTS → INTERPRETATIONS → FEELINGS → ACTIONS

Now consider controlling your interpretation of an event or an encounter with a person from a compassionate viewpoint.

**EVENTS → INTERPRETATIONS with caring curiosity →
COMPASSION → POSITIVE ACTIONS**

Can you imagine that you may have a happier outlook if you see others from the monk's viewpoint versus the lizard's?

The call for showing compassion is nothing new. Over two thousand years ago, Jesus implored his followers to show compassion toward one another—the poor, the ill, the criminal, everyone. Before that, in India, Buddha talked to his students of the importance of opening their hearts to the suffering of the world. In fact, every religion teaches compassion. Perhaps one of the reasons is because treating ourselves and others with compassion just feels good and makes for living in community with others (what we all do, except for hermits!) more peaceful,

calm, and comfortable.

Practicing a compassionate viewpoint connects us with the rest of humanity. When you're curious about why the woman on the street corner is homeless and try to imagine what her day is like, you might be aroused by the feelings of tenderness, sadness, and concern and be moved to volunteer at a soup kitchen. When you see someone sitting alone in the school cafeteria and wonder where his or her friends are, perhaps compassion will trigger you to invite that fellow classmate to join your table of friends.

The benefits of such compassionate acts are abundant. People who practice self-compassion and compassion for others experience less anxiety and depression. Also, those practicing compassion toward others are more relaxed and happier than if they went through life treating others with hate, hostility, indifference, ignorance, or false superiority.

GOOD JUDGMENT VS. BEING JUDGMENTAL

In general, the flip side of being compassionate is being judgmental. Sure, we all "judge" our own and others' choices, lifestyles, situations, and appearance. To have "good" judgment means you can discern facts from opinions, have a strong sense of right from wrong (according to your own value system), and make choices that support your growth. But, being judgmental of ourselves and others shows up as stereotyping, bad-mouthing, and just plain meanness—or worse.

INTERESTING FACT

Having good judgment is different from being judgmental.

When you're judgmental, fear is often at the root. Our inner cave dweller is afraid of anything different, so we immediately find fault with those who are different. We label them as difficult or inferior or bossy or dirty (or . . .) to justify our need to avoid what we're afraid of being near. Granted, "distancing ourselves" is a natural human response; we all have "internal radar" about how close we can allow people, both physically and emotionally. In some cases, this can be a very good thing. For example, you want your "uh oh" feeling to kick in so you can distance yourself from people or situations that evoke unpleasant feelings. But, without examining and labeling the ANTs that creep up when that primitive "uh oh" is triggered, you might not be discerning nor able to relate to others in an understanding manner and, ultimately, see them for the good, although different, people they are.

If we stop ANTs in their tracks and replace them with balanced, realistic thoughts, we might find that the people different from us can teach us something or otherwise enrich our lives. As noted above, this implies that compassion requires the skill of determining what is **fact** and what is **opinion**. For example, a fact is that water is made up of hydrogen and

oxygen. An opinion is that water tastes better than root beer.

Facts are objective information that can be proven in a scientific manner; they hinge on hard evidence. Opinions are subjective, based upon our own personal experiences and preferences. These opinions may be held by many others, but they cannot be proven in a laboratory; rather, they come from our value system, our family background, and our likes and dislikes.

Racial, cultural, and sexual orientation judgments are perfect examples of how subjective opinions might color our judgment of others if we do not attempt to understand those who are dissimilar to us. Consider this: Because we naturally feel comfortable with and have developed our opinions from our own traditions and people, most of us tend to stay within our own groups. When we encounter some-

one outside our "tribe," our inner cave dweller goes on high alert—and lots of different ANTs start to crawl around in our minds, saying things such as: "Because she's wearing a hijab, niqub, or burka, she must be a terrorist." (jumping to conclusions) "He can't speak English. What a dummy!" (black-and-white thinking and labeling) "She is Asian and probably a brain. She wouldn't want to hang out with us; we have nothing in common." (jumping to conclu-

sions, over-generalizing, disqualifying the positive, and labeling) When we don't recognize our ANTs for what they are, we can feel distant, anxious, angry, and uncomfortable. We may show blame, contempt, hostility, or indifference to justify keeping our distance—out of fear.

PUT DOWN THE MAGNIFYING GLASS
AND PICK UP THE MIRROR

There is a theory that many scoff at but that
psychology continues to promote. The theory says
that we judge in others the very characteristics we
do not like about ourselves. For example, we may
judge someone who seems weaker than we are,
because we fear our own weakness. In reaction,
we distance ourselves from our discomfort with
thoughts that we are better than the perceived
weak person. In this way, we don't have to face our
own shortcomings. Accepting our own flaws can be challenging!.

Seeing others with compassion requires the skill to recognize when you
are judging someone for something that is also a part of you. When you
find another's appearance comical or distasteful, you might also have your
own insecurities about the way you look. To accept that others have their
right to their own style or are blessed with other manifestations of beauty
might necessitate you stop saying negative things to yourself.

Even the small annoyances we feel are often for the very things we dislike in ourselves. Think how hard it is to stop biting our fingernails, lose ten
pounds, make and keep lots of friends, always look good, or perform well
athletically. When we are judging others for having bad hair days, missing
a free-throw shot, asking a stupid question in class, or not being asked to
a dance, *we are condemning them for being the same kind of human as each of us...
imperfect.*

When we participate in the alienation of others, we only serve to further
our own alienation. If they are to be ostracized for being imperfect by our
standards, then we will live in fear of being ostracized when we are finally
found out.

What would it say about you if you stopped worrying about how others
behave and worked exclusively on your own transformation? What would
it be like, if every single time you caught yourself judging another, you
asked yourself, "Hey, am I really free of this flaw or similar flaws?" If the
answer is no, take the time to be kind to yourself, and the other person, by
putting the situation in perspective.

STAYING TRUE TO YOU

Some might tell you that to have understanding for someone means that you approve of their behavior. On the contrary, having compassion for others does not equal "agreement." That is, with compassion, we seek to understand the forces that motivate peoples' (including our own) actions, attitudes, behaviors, choices, and perspectives. But that doesn't mean we have to agree with those actions, attitudes, etc. In other words, we can understand and *agree* with a person, but we also can understand and *disagree*. Through true compassion, we may see things differently from each other while, at the same time, understanding and respecting the factors that influence the other's perspective, choices, and lifestyle.

Compassion for others does not require forgoing the standards, morals, and values in which you believe. You don't need to be a pushover! Rather, compassion for others requires the ability to recognize that your way of being, doing things, dressing, eating, or celebrating your faith is just that: your way. In fact, seeing the world from a lens of compassion will make you more certain of who you are and for what you stand.

But compassion is also not about letting anyone off the hook or relieving anyone (including yourself) of the responsibility to make decent behavior choices. Instead, compassion is all about understanding and respecting the forces that affect the situation.

With compassion, the lens with which you view your world is wiped clean of bias, prejudice, and the black-and-white thinking that says you are right and "they" are wrong. With compassion, you dare to see the world from your heart. It allows you to dislike what someone is doing and still recognize that he or she is worthy of respect as a human being, that each of us has a story behind what has led us to make the choices we have made. Until we take the time to see the person behind the differences, the pain, the turmoil—to understand the story—we will never see the humanity in others. We don't necessarily have to do anything to address the issues affecting another; rather, we simply need to bring a compassionate attitude to the interaction.

An example of compassion comes from Mitchell. During the past several months, Mitchell passed a homeless woman on the street near his subway stop. At least one morning each week, Mitchell gave the woman a dollar without actually looking into the woman's face or greeting her in any way. In Civics class one day, the group discussed attitudes toward the poor. Mitchell realized that, although he was showing the homeless woman sympathy by giving her money, he was not really honoring that woman's humanity.

The day after his Civics class, Mitchell again noticed the woman on the street, but this time Mitchell looked at the woman and greeted her, wishing her a good day. Mitchell gave the woman a dollar *and* a smile, looking right into her eyes. This time the interaction felt like compassion. Mitchell had exhibited understanding and respect. The interaction—although more difficult, because Mitchell was afraid of his own guilt and judgmental thoughts—felt authentic and personally rewarding to Mitchell.

SELF-COMPASSION

While working on compassion for others is important, having compassion for yourself is as well. Most people are too hard on themselves, usually out of a drive to improve performance. Ironically, the more you disqualify your positives, the more likely you are to have low self-esteem, and the less motivated you are to try your best.

Many of us make the mistake of internalizing the messages we receive about being failures (personalization, mind reading, and labeling), or even misinterpret the comments of parents or teachers about the need to improve. We may believe those messages are about our value, acceptability, or worth, rather than simply about our performance. To have compassion for yourself is to notice the ANTs of self-judgments and replace them with a balanced view of your character. In other words, engage your inner monk and treat yourself with understanding and wisdom.

SELF-COMPASSION

"[W]e need a way to know ourselves gently, without judgment, without displeasure. We need to find a way to look at our discomfort, agitation, restlessness, boredom, and insecurities. We need a way to look at ourselves and accept ourselves just as we are. Only then will we learn to love ourselves and stop running away. When we begin to watch ourselves, it is as though we have a second person watching our mind's work. It is as though we have developed a gentle witness who does not get caught up in our soap operas, who does not become a news commentator, and who does not judge our thoughts or actions as right or wrong. This witness becomes like a best friend, someone who is always there and just is with us—a friend who notices and points out, but doesn't judge."

- Ruth Fishel

One way to look at the process of thinking compassionately toward yourself is to imagine a part of your brain (the monk) observing you with the same fondness and acceptance as your best friend might. You can even name this part of your brain something like "Angel" or "Wise One" or "Mr. Understanding." This part of your brain understands why you do what you do. There are no ANTs in this part of the brain. If this part is in use, it is completely free of negativity. This part doesn't get caught up in the dramas of your life, doesn't judge you, and is able to observe your thoughts, feelings, and choices. It can guide you back to thinking and acting in balanced ways. The more you turn to this part of your brain to guide your view of your self, the more you will automatically turn this view toward others.

Do you think it's silly to need compassion? One common ANT about needing compassion is that you shouldn't need it ("should" statement). Some people feel it's a sign of weakness to need compassion from themselves or others. The same is true of the idea that you need to love yourself. You might think it is ridiculous and a bunch of fluff to love yourself, but actually it's a normal part of good self-esteem. Loving yourself and having compassion for your struggles and shortcomings will help to motivate you to greatness much better than beating up yourself.

CHANGE YOUR MIND, CHANGE YOUR WORLD

During your teenage years is the perfect time to cultivate compassion. That's because, during this time, you're rebuilding all the connections in your brain, readying your mind for adulthood. In fact, this natural time of pruning old thought patterns is the easiest time to create your own view of the world. Because having compassionate thoughts for yourself and others leads to feelings of care, concern, love, and tenderness, you will be motivated to act on those feelings instead of getting mired down in anger, blame, overgeneralizing, bad conclusions, and negative judgments. Compassion takes the worldview that we are all basically good and trying our best to be even better. It's the key for increasing our positive effect on our surrounding environment. Compassion is the means for ending our day feeling truly connected to each other and positive about ourselves. It's the answer to the great emptiness inside many of us.

Take the information contained in this book and make a difference! It's your mind: Own it. Change it. And you can change your life. Change your life, and you can change the world!

In order to do the hard, but invaluable, work of developing a compassionate viewpoint, remember to do the following:

- **Observe your thoughts:** Slow down, notice the story you are telling yourself, and breathe.
- **Monitor your thoughts for ANTs:** Pay attention to the thinking behind your judgment. Is it valid? Label any thinking errors you notice.
- **Replace the ANTs with a viewpoint of compassion:** Replace the judgment of others with curiosity about what motivates their behavior. Replace judgment of yourself with the best friend treatment. Ask yourself, "Would I say this to my best friend in the same situation? If not, what would I say?"

Don't look now, but you are developing an inner monk! In the next few chapters, we'll share with you even more ideas that can help you to "own" your mind—such as tips on getting motivated, inspiration for turning failure into success, and suggestions for staying the course and creating a life you love.

REST STOP

REMEMBERING
Key words and phrases: Can you define them?

Facts versus Opinions _____

_____

Compassionate Viewpoint _____

_____

Consciousness Central _____

_____

Being Your Own Best Friend _____

_____

REFLECTING
Take time to ponder the following.

What are your value judgments about compassion?

_____

_____

_____

_____

What are some situations in which you were very compassionate? What are some situations in which you were not compassionate? Why did you respond differently?

_____

_____

_____

_____

REINFORCING

Try these exercises to reinforce what you've learned.

1) Rate the following statements regarding whether they are facts (F) or opinions (O). Then think about why you responded as you did.

- People shouldn't show their anger. (F/O)
- People will think I am foolish if I express my needs. (F/O)
- People will kick you when you are down. (F/O)
- Forests are necessary for clean air. (F/O)
- It's cool to be a movie star. (F/O)
- It's easier to be happy when you're rich than when you're poor. (F/O)
- It's always better to be thin than to be heavy. (F/O)
- Feelings follow thoughts within five seconds. (F/O)
- People are basically good. (F/O)
- People are basically bad. (F/O)
- You can't really trust anyone over 25 years of age. (F/O)
- Your biggest asset for good self-esteem is your brain. (F/O)

2) List five flaws for which you would give compassion to another, but not to yourself.

_____

_____

_____

_____

_____

3) On a separate sheet of paper, make a list of the behaviors, traits, and past situations for which you harbor judgments of yourself. Next to each item answer this question: "What would I tell my best friend if he or she had this dilemma?" Using this same list of judgments, read through each item and label any ANTs.

4) List at least three people about whom you hold judgments such as someone you're dating or a classmate who annoys you. Under each name, generate as long a list as you can of their positive character traits, their lovable or kind behaviors, their positive physical characteristics, and their innate goodness. In the weeks ahead, practice dwelling on the positives. Each time you catch yourself noticing something negative about someone, wipe your mind clean and filter for positives. Catch people doing things right!

RECORDING AND RESOLVING

Journal writing is a great tool for learning how to control your thoughts and feelings.

Keep a judgment journal for one week. Write down the instances in which you judge yourself or another, and those in which you observe others' judgments. Read through your journal entries and ask yourself, "Are these facts or are these opinions?" Then, read through the journal entries concerning your own judgments. Apply the following question to each judgment: "What could I be curious about that would replace this judgment?" For example, you thought, "Look at that idiot. He went right through that stop sign." Replacing this judgment with curiosity might sound like this: "Whoa, that was scary. I wonder why he didn't stop at the sign."

_____

_____

_____

_____

_____

_____

_____

_____

_____

_____

_____

_____

_____

_____

Go through the day tomorrow with the intention of observing
yourself and the world as a monk. Keep journal notes about
what you notice.

_____
_____
_____
_____
_____
_____
_____
_____
_____
_____
_____
_____
_____
_____
_____
_____
_____
_____
_____
_____
_____
_____

Remember:

EVENTS → INTERPRETATIONS → FEELINGS → ACTIONS

GETTING MOTIVATED

Getting motivated is hard, and we've all struggled with it at one time or another. Although we might have a long list of things we want to do, **goals** we hope to accomplish, or undone tasks nagging us, we can't seem to get started. In fact, even when we know something is important, might be good for us, or that we'll really suffer if we don't make an effort, many of us often fall into the rut of actively not trying. In fact, too often we use our strong will to *refuse* to take action, rather than to get moving. True confession: When we started to write this manual, we both knew our biggest obstacle would be procrastination!

Of course, some pesky ANTs can prevent us from getting started and sabotage us when we are under way. But two other issues might crop up when you attempt to get yourself in gear: First, you might lack necessary skills, or, second, you might not understand how your **impetus**, or drive, to accomplish goals actually works. The type of skills that help people become and stay motivated differ with the challenge at hand. Skills such as organization and self-discipline are useful in any pursuits, but for many goals you may need skills such as how to research information, use money wisely, prepare for a job interview, or overcome your fear of asking for help. When you don't have all the skills needed for accomplishing your goal, you could get bogged down in the details—and the challenge.

Motivated people often have resources and allies that help them stay on task and acquire the needed skills. The allies might even back them with rides, financial support, and encouragement. In our highest ideals, we often think of motivated people succeeding all on their own, but that's rarely the case.

Understanding where your motivation comes from and how it gets stalled is the first step in harnessing your tremendous power to achieve the life you want. Let's look at the origins of motivation and some skills most motivated people have in common.

MOTIVATION 101

There are two types of motivation: internal and external. **Internally motivated** people tend to work toward success because they want to feel good about themselves. When they accomplish a goal, they feel a sense of satisfaction and competence. And the feeling is the reward itself. People acknowledged for having a "strong will" are often internally motivated.

External motivation is driven by a perceived or real reward from outside oneself. It's the old "carrot on a stick" concept. The external rewards might consist of approval from one's culture or family, material gain such as a good grade or a pay raise, increased popularity with peers, or avoidance of punishment or disapproval. Those who are primarily externally motivated tend to lose some interest in attaining their goals when the reward has passed or is withheld.

You might find that using both internal and external motivators can provide a healthy balance. Also, what motivates you can change over time. For example, you might initially read your literature book because you will receive a poor grade and be grounded if you don't (external), but then you might discover you love the book (internal) and feel proud of the grade you receive on the book report (internal). The following example from Darius may illustrate how a balance of motivations works and how what motivates you can shift over time.

Darius is an 18-year-old senior at Evergreen High School. He was born with a congenital disorder that left him unable to walk. From the time Darius was a little boy, he was strongwilled and determined to succeed. It's no surprise he is the class president, valedictorian, and a volunteer for the after-school tutoring program. He also plays in a citywide basketball league for disabled people and has competed in several notable wheelchair races. Recently, he was accepted at an Ivy League college, where he's the recipient of a significant scholarship.

Darius has a variety of factors motivating him. Darius wants to succeed so people see more than his disability; this is external motivation, because he cares what others think. He also seeks to avoid judgment and pity (external); he wants to show the world he is not disabled, that he just cannot walk. Plus, he is proud he was accepted at a prestigious college without the admissions staff knowing his race or his disability (external).

On the other hand, Darius is also internally motivated because he feels good when he competes and wins. He loves getting his report card because it reinforces how great he feels about himself (internal). He loves racing and playing basketball because he can make his body perform (internal). And he feels good about his body working well, even if no one else notices (internal).

Darius is also motivated to exercise because he loves junk food. He knows that, because he's in a wheelchair, he could easily develop a weight problem if he doesn't get out there and burn calories. Because he loves ice cream, candy bars, and chips with salsa, he has to burn lots of calories! Darius' motivation in this regard is both internal and external. He doesn't want to get too heavy because he wants to look good (external), but he also wants to feel good (internal) and knows that getting heavy will jeopardize his overall health.

PLEASURE AND PAIN: COMMON INCENTIVES

Two very common **incentives** are pleasure and pain. Both can be either internal or external. Individuals may be more motivated by pleasure and, therefore, entice themselves to complete goals so they allow themselves a reward. For example, a person who tells herself she can watch a movie after she gets her paper written is being motivated by pleasure.

Withholding pleasure or punishing oneself is an example of being motivated by pain. When you tell yourself you can't go out tonight because you didn't finish your History homework, or your parents ground you because you didn't do your chores, that's motivation (or attempted motivation) by pain.

Some equate motivation by pain with **delayed gratification**, or resisting the temptation for an immediate reward and waiting for a more worthwhile reward. For example, by putting off texting your friend until you're done practicing the guitar can reap huge benefits; with dedicated practice, you might become the next Jimi Hendrix! Truly, learning how to wait for and work toward what you want is crucial for success. Life, in general, can be hard, and accomplishing tasks and goals can be demanding. When you develop your "disappointment muscle" by accepting little disappointments in your days, you eventually build up the confidence that you can set goals and reach them, and that you can even tackle huge hardships. A growing body of literature also has linked the ability to delay gratification to specific positive outcomes such as academic success and physical health. In other words, if you can motivate yourself by accepting some pain (not being able to go out with a friend, not being able to watch TV, not being able to eat that chocolate bar, etc.), you might more readily do well in school and excel at your sport or creative endeavor.

MOTIVATION STOPPERS

As you attempt to motivate yourself, you may tell yourself you're a good person if you finish your chores (pleasure) or that you're a loser if you avoid going out and finding a job (pain). Warning: Utilizing negative thoughts about yourself for motivation can be self-defeating and **counterproductive**, stopping you from reaching your goals rather than helping. So, it's important to observe how you use inner dialogue to motivate yourself.

ANTs can create some of your biggest motivation stoppers. "Should," "ought to," and "must" thoughts (the Family of Shoulds) can awaken within you an **inner rebel** who may resist cooperating. This inner rebel can throw a tantrum and refuse to do what even you are dictating must be done, causing you to **procrastinate**, or put off what needs to be done until later. When you attempt to use the "Family of Shoulds" to motivate yourself, you can feel like a "victim of opportunity," obliged to perform. This is not healthy and not a good recipe for accomplishment. Rather, you perform best in life when you feel you are freely choosing to take action—and that action appears to be in your best interest. Every time you tell yourself you "must" or "should" do something, you're taking away your sense of free choice.

Other ANTs that often prevent us from motivation are overgeneralization ("I never get anything done anyway, so why bother?") and jumping to conclusions ("I'm going to fail anyway, so why bother?"). Fear-generating thoughts are another mental pitfall when we need to be motivated. Telling yourself "I'm not up to the task" (disqualifying the positive) or "people will laugh at me" (jumping to conclusions) will likely lead to a feeling of anxiety, which can cause **behavioral paralysis**. In other words, you feel stuck and do nothing.

BACK OFF!

Few of us have escaped criticism and nagging by often well-meaning adults regarding our lack of motivation. They may have believed they were making an observation of our behavior based on facts, when, in fact, they were evaluating or sharing an opinion about our behavior. All too often we are told we are lazy, underachievers, or not living up to our potential. Generally, another's evaluation is meant to be helpful, yet, as most of us know, this is anything but!

Take the case of Rachel, a 16-year-old junior at Park Ridge High School. Rachel is usually a B student and typical in her habits, meaning she works hard at times and less so at other times. Lately, Rachel has taken up two new pastimes: She's dating Kevin, and she's discovered snowboarding. She manages to get to the mountain nearly every weekend, and, although her grades were strong in the fall, she has received three poor progress reports during the second quarter. A "motivational" interchange with her father follows:

Mr. Cruz: "Rachel! What the heck's going on? You're failing History and French and have a D in Math! You'd better have a good explanation for this, young lady!"

Rachel: "Relax, Dad. You're overreacting. I'm a little behind. That's all. I handed in some stuff late, but I'm caught up in French now. It's cool. I've got it under control."

Mr. Cruz: "All of a sudden, you're so lazy. I can't believe you would slack off like this in your junior year. You should be working harder, not doing less. Olivia never squandered her time. Your sister was working hard on her grades when she was your age. If you want to go to college, you've got to start working harder. This is plain laziness."

(*Rachel thinks to herself:* "I really should have been working harder, but it's probably too late now anyway. I've sunk too low; I'll never get out of this hole. I'm not like Olivia; I can't work like she does.")

Rachel: "I'm sick of being compared to perfect Olivia who never messes up. I'm not as smart as she is, and I always disappoint you guys anyway."

Mr. Cruz: "You are just as smart as your sister. You just don't apply yourself. You are so unmotivated. But I'm going to motivate you. Until you get everything caught up and your grades where they were, you aren't going out with Kevin, and your lift ticket is going in my wallet. Now park that snowboard and hit the books!"

After another five minutes of back-and-forth blame, anger, and frustration, Rachel slams off to her room. And it doesn't stop there for Rachel. She still can't get herself going. By now she is so full of anger and self-loathing that she can't concentrate, so she makes the next mistake of thinking, "I'm just not in the mood to study. I'll just lie here and check my phone until I feel like doing my math." Oh, no! Another ANT! All-or-nothing thinking can push us right into the trap of "The situation is perfect," "The situation is terrible," or "I don't feel like doing this task, so I'll wait until I suddenly *feel* like doing it," the all-or-nothing quandary. It's frequently a thinking error to believe you will eventually feel like doing something you have been putting off. Remember, feelings follow thoughts! Unless you *think* your way into feeling like doing something, your stagnation usually won't change on its own.

Getting back to Rachel. . . . She does want to succeed. Even in all her distress, she reminds herself she wants to go to college. (Probably, in part, to get away from her parents!) Her trouble is that she tries to motivate herself through her **inner critic** who shares only negative self-evaluations, but this form of coercion doesn't work. Instead, it awakens a tantrum from her inner rebel! So she lies down on the bed and posts snowboarding pictures while the inner critic continues trying to motivate her through threats and criticism, making the problem worse.

ON THE RIGHT TRACK

So, what's the solution? What are the healthy and effective ways to motivate you? First, we will look at combating the ANTs, and then we will share with you some strategies for getting motivated.

First, the ANTS: As with any ANT, the trick is always to notice the self-defeating thought, recognize the thinking error involved (label it), and replace it with a balanced and realistic thought. Let's look at Rachel's ANTs and follow the steps to ANT control.

Rachel told herself, "I should be working harder." This, of course, is a "should" statement, and "should" statements backfire by robbing us of a feeling of free choice and making us feel guilty, depressed, and unmotivated. A balanced, realistic thought might be, "I could have been studying more, but I chose not to and now I'm behind. Maybe it's time to start spending more time on homework, because I didn't like those progress reports. I want to do well in school. I just want to have some fun, too."

Rachel's inner critic labeled her "lazy" and a "failure," but, once Rachel noticed this, she could remember to tell herself, "I am not lazy. I get up every day at 5:45 to get to school by 7:00. I'm always on the go. Kevin and I go out a lot and get to the mountain every week. Snowboarding is not a lazy person's sport. It's hard work. Plus, I work two evenings a week, do all my laundry, and clean both bathrooms. I'm not a failure either. I've gotten on the honor roll every semester since I started middle school. I just haven't applied myself lately. My priorities may need adjusting, but I am not a lazy failure."

So many times we get defensive when someone else points out our flaws, but, when it comes to that inner critic, we're quick to agree. If we spent the same amount of energy disputing the inner critic's claims that most of us spend arguing with authorities, we would have perfect self-esteem! We are fighting the wrong battle. Months or years of beating ourselves up for procrastination will negatively affect our self-esteem. In fact, a core component of good self-esteem is living up to our own standards.

> **INTERESTING FACT**
>
> A core componenet of good self-esteem is living up to your own standards.

If we feel guilty or angry that we've let ourselves down in the past, we will judge and dislike ourselves.

Guess what? None of us lives up to our standards 100% of the time. You have to be able to adopt an attitude that reminds you to move on from past failures. Low self-esteem keeps you from trying as hard as you can right now, because low self-esteem causes disinterest and inactivity.

In Rachel's self-talk, there were examples of predicting the future, mind reading, and personalization. She told herself she would never do as well as her sister Olivia, that she was a huge disappointment to her parents, and that it was too late to salvage her grades. If she caught these ANTs marching through her mind, she might replace them with balanced thoughts such as the following: "My parents are upset with my grades, but they are usually very proud of me. My mom is always telling me how much she loves me, and my dad just doesn't know what to do to get me going. I don't know if it's too late or not, but I could make a list of the work that's due and go and talk to my teachers. If it's too late for this semester, I can focus on working harder next semester and bring my grades back up."

Lastly, but very importantly, Rachel can catch herself in the all-or-nothing thinking that tells her, "I'm not in the mood to study. I'll have to wait until I'm in the mood." Bad idea. What do you think the chances are that the mood to study will visit Rachel like some fairy sprinkling "study dust" on her head? Probably not very good. Waiting until a mood strikes us is a dreadful ANT trap. A more realistic thought would be, "The mood won't just sneak up on me. Most likely, if I take some action, I will get going and feel more motivated. Small actions will lead to more action. If I can't concentrate on math right now, I can at least make my list of assignments." In other words, provide your own magic dust!

MOTIVATION SECRETS

Get to know your motivation style. Are you internally motivated or externally motivated? Motivated by pain or pleasure? Punishment or rewards? Would working out small ways to reward yourself each step of the way help or would withholding the goodies until you do all the deeds work better for you? Do you need to be accountable to someone other than yourself each day or week, or are you more motivated by being honest with yourself? It's important to know *your own mind*, how *you're* put together, in order to get the most from yourself. The key is *self-truthfulness*.

Have a mission statement, or personal vision, that serves as a motivating force. Look at yourself and ask, "Who am I really? How do I show up in life? What are my goals?" Examine your own desires, values, and beliefs without concerning yourself with what others may want for you. Many times what our culture, our parents, or our best friends want for us isn't compatible with our internal goals. Everyone also needs to know where "me" begins and the outside influences end. That is, being "good" cannot always motivate us; we also have a need to be motivated by being "real," or authentic. Then, when our external motivators fail us, we have internal ones upon which to rely. It's like having an inner compass and knowing your "true North." In other words, only you know when and/or if to use pleasure or pain as a motivator, or how to use one goal to motivate you in other areas.

For example, Rachel has the goal of being a good snowboarder. It isn't her only goal, but it is one she can use to motivate herself by either pain or pleasure. ("If I get my work done this week, I can go to the mountain. If my homework is not done by Friday night, I will choose to stay home over the weekend and do homework.") In this way, she is using one of her goals to motivate her to accomplish the others.

Set reasonable, realistic goals and learn how to reach them by breaking them down into specific tasks. Once you have goals, turn them into a series of specific steps and then into specific **tasks**, or actions you can take. Review and revise your plan often. Praise yourself for the smallest accomplishment. It's from small bricks and stones that the great cathedrals were built—one at a time.

It's also important to review your goals and check off tasks regularly. This will remind you of your successes and, ultimately, enable you to assess continually whether you are on the right track. Keeping the end goal in mind also allows you to focus your energy on moving forward rather than on the ANTs that steal your precious energy and prevent you from reaching your end goal. Think of ANTs as the roadblocks that get in the way of your natural motivation to move toward a goal.

INTERESTING FACT

Small actions will lead to more action.

Check the stories you tell yourself. You know, the ANTs! Turn your "shoulds" into "coulds." Avoid the ANT traps, because they only invite reactions from the inner critic or the inner rebel.

Use the tool of creative visualization. This is the practice of attempting to affect your "outer" life by using your imagination to visualize specific behaviors or events. The idea is that, if you visualize a desire over and over again with all your senses, you can attain your goal. For example, in sports, a basketball player might visualize the perfect free throw over and over again to mentally train muscle memory. This increases the chance that the player's muscle memory will come through in the clutch moment of a big game.

The technique of creative visualization involves thinking in your "mind's eye" what reaching your goal looks like, feels like, sounds like, even smells like! In essence, creative visualization rewires your subconscious patterns. T. Harv Eker, author of *Secrets of the Millionaire Mind*, says, "It all comes down to this: If your subconscious 'blueprint' is not 'set' for success, nothing you learn, nothing you know, and nothing you do will make much of a difference. . . . By changing your subconscious programming, you take the first essential step to changing your result." This means that the key to creating lasting, positive change in your life is through the rewiring of your subconscious patterns—and that means getting off the ANT highway and thinking positive thoughts!

Ask yourself if you really believe you deserve success. If the answer is no, then search for the core beliefs and ANTs at work in your negative assessment. Turn those core beliefs into good self-worth. When you know to the core of your being that you are worthwhile, you strive for more.

Here's an interesting way to look at self-worth: Imagine that, at birth, each individual received one unit of worth. No one on Earth received more or less than one unit. Throughout life, you cannot lose that unit nor sell it; you cannot buy more nor have it taken away. It's yours, and you didn't have to earn it. It was factory installed! Your job while living is to manage and utilize that unit instead of worrying that you don't have any—but that the star basketball player you envy has six!

> **When you know to the core of your being that you are worthwhile, you strive for more.**

Here's how you manage it:

- Pay attention to it.
- Keep it polished.
- If it gets tarnished, think about what you need to do to make it shiny again.

Do not be afraid to ask for help. If you don't know how to discipline yourself, ask someone who does know. To organize and motivate oneself is not necessarily natural. Look around yourself and see who seems to be motivated. Then get over your ego and ask for pointers. Some of the tips will work and will stick with you for a lifetime.

Do not be afraid to make mistakes. Did you know that Einstein once flunked math? Most likely every individual you admire made a lot of mistakes along the way. In fact, if you want to be a person who lives a full and

"It's not that I'm so smart; it's just that I stay with problems longer."
– Albert Einstein

satisfying life, you will have to make a minimum of five mistakes every day. If you only make four today, you'll have to make six tomorrow! We're kidding, but you do need to watch for the ANTs that generate fear and put them in their place. This is such an incredibly important point that we're going to devote the entire next chapter to the positive power of failure.

REST STOP

REMEMBERING
Key words and phrases: Can you define them?

Procrastination

Internal Motivation

External Motivation

Inner Critic

Inner Rebel _____

_____

Incentive _____

_____

Behavioral Paralysis _____

_____

Goals _____

_____

Tasks _____

_____

Counterproductive _____

_____

Impetus _____

_____

Mission Statement _____

_____

Delayed Gratification _____

_____

Creative Visualization _____

_____

REFLECTING
Take time to ponder the following.

What do you believe in? When you are at your best, how do you see yourself? For what would you like to stand? How do you want to show up in the world? Consider questions such as this and then create a personal mission statement. You might even come up with a t-shirt or bumper sticker design that reflects your personal mission statement.

_____

_____

_____

_____

_____

Sometimes people get stuck because of something from their past they haven't gotten over yet. Whatever it is has become an obstacle to starting or trying again. Is there something from your past that gets in the way of your motivation? If you suspect there is something keeping you down, analyze it by finishing the following statements.

An incident I have trouble forgiving myself for is _____

_____

The damage I caused myself is_____

_____

The reason I may have acted this way is _____

_____

My standard I didn't live up to is _____

_____

How I would have liked to do it differently is _____

_____

Now and in the future, the behavior of mine I would like to change

is _____

_____

An action I may need to take to put this behind me is _____

_____

After completing the writing exercise, consider if there is anyone with whom you would like to share your discoveries.

REINFORCING
Try these exercises to reinforce what you've learned.

1) Re-read Rachel's story and label her ANTs, the common ones we have identified in this manual and any you find on your own. Write them down on a separate piece of paper. Then note times over the past two weeks that you have engaged in or witnessed these same faulty thoughts in yourself. Describe those times and write out how you might have turned your negative thoughts into balanced ones.

2) Interview one person whom you greatly respect and discuss the idea of "motivation." Write down on a separate sheet of paper ideas from that person you think may be beneficial to you.

3) List your family members and beside each name write one method you know that family member uses to self-motivate. Note who you think reaches their goals most often.

_____

_____

_____

RECORDING AND RESOLVING

Journal writing is a great tool for learning how to control your thoughts and feelings.

Because this exercise takes up a lot of paper, you may want to use your own journal. (Use this space to doodle, if you like.)

Make a "Goals Chart" in a journal. In the first column, list your goals, both personal and school-related. Did you include goals for having fun? Goals that will make you grow? Goals to help you connect with others? And goals that will help you to find solitude? What else?

In the second column of your chart, note what motivates or might motivate you to reach each goal. In the third column, identify if that motivator is pain or pleasure. Then, in a fourth column, identify if that motivator is internal or external. That is, ask yourself: Why are these goals important to me? Are they attempts at gaining approval or to make me feel good about myself, to be true to myself? Finally, in the last column of your chart, identify the possible negative effects of the ways in which you attempt to motivate yourself.

Once you have your chart made, list each goal on a separate page. For each, consider what steps you need to reach your goal, and list those steps under the goal. Then, break each step into tasks and list those tasks.

Over the course of two weeks, review your Goals Chart and goal outlines daily, checking off the tasks and steps you have completed. Journal about your progress and any ANTs that arise as you work toward the goals. Be sure you label and replace the ANTs! Although goals may make others happy as well, try to focus on your self-interest for each goal. Is each one a free choice?

Once you've completed a goal, take that goal outline and rip it in pieces, discarding it. Congratulate yourself for your accomplishment!

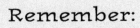

Remember:

EVENTS → INTERPRETATIONS → FEELINGS → ACTIONS

FINDING SUCCESS IN FAILURE

Think back to a time when you hit an unexpected roadblock or experienced a different outcome than you were expecting. Maybe you didn't do as well on a test as you would have liked, or you didn't run as fast a time in your track meet as you had hoped, or you tried to get attention from a certain someone and it backfired. In these types of situations, labeling the outcome of the event—or even yourself—as "a failure" can be tempting. What you may not recognize, though, is that what we usually label as failures are basically thinking errors; they are failures only in our own minds or just because we say so. Another thing you may not recognize is that failure doesn't have to be a bad thing anyway! Consider the Wright brothers' first airplanes that crashed on the beach.

Although our society places much emphasis on the idea of succeeding, many great successes would never have happened without failure. Alexander Fleming discovered penicillin when he left a messy lab desk and returned to find mold growing; Martin Luther King Jr. couldn't summon enough people for his civil rights marches in Birmingham in 1963, but, when his team happened to schedule one at work quitting time, the streets overflowed. Also, Thomas Edison, now celebrated as one of the world's greatest inventors, tried to invent the light bulb at least a thousand times before he came up with a successful prototype. He later wrote that he had not failed one thousand times, but that he had just "found one thousand ways that did not work." Whether labeled as "failures" or not, Edison's attempts to invent the light bulb illustrate why the process of "try-and-try-again" is so important: When things don't go right, you can adapt and learn from your experiences.

In truth, failures aren't setbacks. Rather, they're opportunities for growth. What might be labeled a failure also represents an opportunity to summon a different kind of creativity that might elicit an outcome even more awesome than the original vision! For example, have you ever accidentally deleted an English assignment on your computer (arghh!), only to rewrite it and find that the second version was much better? Been there; done that!

Unfortunately, when you resist the idea of failure, you become attached to your original vision in a way that is ultimately unhelpful. Instead of unhelpful **attachment**, we might strive for **commitment**. Buddhists have a concept describing the difference between attachment and commitment. According to this belief,

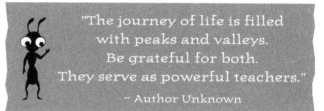

"The journey of life is filled with peaks and valleys. Be grateful for both. They serve as powerful teachers."
– Author Unknown

when we are *attached* to something, we keep attempting to create it into a certain form or mold; our vision, inevitably, is most often far too small for the full possibility of what it could become. On the other hand, when we are *committed* to something, we get to control our part in how we tend to it, practice it, and dedicate ourselves to it. When we are committed, we maintain a curiosity about what might emerge. This doesn't mean we do not have preferences for the direction we want things to go. Rather, we put our best forward, and we know what we can and cannot control.

THE PROBLEM WITH BEING AFRAID TO FAIL

For many young people, especially teens and pre-teens who label themselves as perfectionists, failure doesn't feel like an option. Sometimes people become so terrified of failing that they won't let themselves take any risks. As a result, they miss out on chances to learn, grow, and contribute to the new ideas and new inventions that can only come from taking a risk. Consider these scenarios:

- Rowan is taking an Algebra class, and his teacher asks if anyone wants to try to solve a problem on the board. Rowan raises his hand because he believes he has the answer, but he gets it wrong. Embarrassed about making a mistake, he doesn't raise his hand in that class for the rest of the semester (all-or-nothing thinking).

• Jema has never played basketball on a team, but she has a hoop in her backyard and practices shooting sometimes. She's thought about trying out for her high school's basketball team, but she knows some of the girls on the team have been playing for years. She worries she won't be able to play as well as they do (jumping to conclusions).

• Riza is a high school senior and straight-A student who plans to go to college. She has done some research on Brown University and thinks she might like to go there. Because she doesn't think her SAT scores are good enough, she doesn't bother applying (filtering).

In all the above examples, the individuals missed opportunities because their ANTs caused them to view a certain possible outcome (e.g., not getting into Brown) as "wrong" or too risky or embarrassing—and, therefore, undesirable. Because of this, these kids may have missed out on not only the outcomes they wanted (learning to do math equations successfully, making the basketball team, getting into Brown), but also on the opportunity to respond to and learn from different outcomes. If they had been *committed* to fully experiencing the process of an endeavor, rather than been *attached* to only the one outcome, amazing things might have occurred.

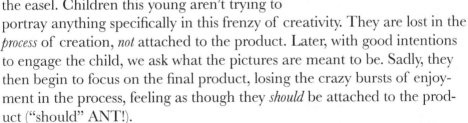

To put this in perspective, think about how brave we all were when we were young! Preschool-aged children create huge volumes of art; one wild painting after another flies off the brush and onto the easel. Children this young aren't trying to portray anything specifically in this frenzy of creativity. They are lost in the *process* of creation, *not* attached to the product. Later, with good intentions to engage the child, we ask what the pictures are meant to be. Sadly, they then begin to focus on the final product, losing the crazy bursts of enjoyment in the process, feeling as though they *should* be attached to the product ("should" ANT!).

Similarly, in order to connect with the flow of creating a life, we all need ample time to get lost in the process of discovery or creation. In other words, find your inner preschooler and play! Other than a good night's sleep, nothing restores our spirit, our creative juices, our energy stores, and our upbeat mood as much as play—which is important not just for little children but for all ages. Let go and follow where your energy goes! There are no mistakes in play, because play is about fun and relaxation. Play is the activity that recharges your battery and helps you to work at your life from the most creative angles.

LETTING GO OF PERFECTIONISM

The people who have the hardest time accepting failure are those who constantly push themselves to achieve success based on standards set by other people. These **perfectionists** are often driven by a fear of failure. While this might motivate them to succeed in some arenas (e.g., grades, sports, artistic endeavors, etc.), the fear of failure often creates an unhealthy amount of stress that will have negative effects in the long run. (Consider: Perfectionists rarely find time to play.)

Do you have perfectionist tendencies? Think about your ANTs! You may be resisting failure and missing opportunities if you:

☐ Engage in a lot of all-or-nothing thinking (e.g., "This way of doing things is right; this way is wrong.")
☐ Always do your best in order to please other people (mind reading, disqualifying the positive).
☐ Compare yourself to others, such as your classmates or an older sibling (possibly disqualifying the positive, labeling).
☐ Procrastinate or avoid things you don't think you're good at (all-or-nothing, disqualifying the positive).
☐ Obsess over little mistakes (catastrophizing).
☐ Take criticism or a bad grade as a personal attack (personalization).
☐ Feel you've never quite reached the level of success you want ("shoulds").

One of the biggest problems with perfectionist thinking is that it leads to impossible expectations. Let's say Reese has an older brother who is a great  musician. He plays the cello, and she plays the violin. But she feels as though she'll never be as good a musician as he is, no matter how much she practices. What she doesn't realize is that she's creating a false competition, as though only one person can be extremely good at something. Because she's so focused on seeing the "perfect" in her brother, she's failing to discover the "perfect" in herself (disqualifying the positive, all-or-nothing thinking). Until she lets go of this mental stumbling block, she will not be able to create her own path, reach her own expectations, or make her own breakthroughs.

> **INTERESTING FACT**
>
> **It's very seductive to try to be "the best" versus "the best I can be."**

There is yet another and often unexamined cost of perfectionism: As long as you believe someone else's "perfect" should be your perfect, you will never be able to expand into a new invention, idea, or possibility. In perfectionistic thinking, you project on others a level of accomplishment that may or may not be true and, in so doing, create barriers to your own attempts. Whereas there's nothing wrong with competition through dedication to a sport, idea, craft, or other activity, pursuit of a high level of competence *entirely based on comparisons* to other people is unhealthy. More than one person can be really good at something at the same time. It's very seductive to try to be "the best" versus "the best I can be."

CULTIVATING A DEDICATED HEART

If we let go of the idea of perfection, then what is the benefit of any practice? And what about the old adage, "Practice makes perfect?" We do not have to throw away the best of "striving"! It's true that only a few of us will ever compete in the Olympics, perform at Carnegie Hall, have our own TV show, have our paintings exhibited at the Guggenheim, or play for the NFL. These results are wonderful for the few who actually achieve them, but, for the rest of us, the practice itself can cultivate within us that which is perhaps even more valuable than fleeting notoriety: a **dedicated heart**. A dedicated heart is a state of mind and a lifestyle of fanning the fires of our inter-

ests and passions. Dedication along with its companion "discipline," once cultivated, can be used to focus on any goal and to create the life we desire.

Those lucky people who wake up most days with excitement about the work and activities of their day are those who have designed a life that they are living **"on purpose."** They have dedicated their heart and their energy to endeavors that have important meaning to them (internal motivation!) Are these happy, fulfilled people all brain surgeons, rock stars, and athletes? Heck no! They are the baristas who love making the cool little flourish in the latte foam. They are the teachers who are totally excited about growing sunflowers with second graders. They are the people who collect coins, and they are the ones who are going to save the planet with alternative energy. They are the lucky ones who know it takes a dedicated heart to make a life worth living. They aren't obsessed with being perfect. They are obsessed with *being*.

DON'T JUST BELIEVE IN IT...BELIEVE IN YOU!

There is a saying, "Peacock today, feather duster tomorrow." If we look to others to define our own successes and failures, we are on a constant

"It's about being the very best you can be. Nothing else matters as long as you're working and striving to be YOUR best."

– Pete Carroll

teeter-totter. One day we can be lifted up with the good opinion of others and then the next day get smacked down when they withdraw their approval.

Think fickle friends. Granted, we need to be concerned about what others think about us to a certain degree; in fact, our brains are hardwired to value the good opinion of others. As adolescents, the opinions of our peers are especially important, often even more so than the opinions of our families. But this doesn't mean the opinions of others must completely govern how we live our lives.

At the end of the day, our lives belong only to us. What we have done or not done is ours alone. Even the people who *most* influence us, challenge us, celebrate or encourage us are the owners of their own lives—and we are left with our own self. Sure, we can appreciate when we are celebrated and be bummed when we're criticized. But, ultimately, we need to believe that others' opinions aren't what define us. If we just be our best selves,

then there is no failure and we can take ourselves off the teeter-totter of comparison and approval (of personalization).

As a case in point, before becoming the coach of the Seattle Seahawks, Pete Carroll was fired by the New England Patriots as well as the New York Jets! Even so, he led the Seattle Seahawks to dominate in the 2013 Super Bowl. An optimist, Carroll challenges each member of his team to believe in himself and to believe in one another. He tells his players, "It's about being the very best you can be. Nothing else matters as long as you're working and striving to be *your* best."

OWN IT!

Anyone who has ever contributed greatness to the world at some point made a decision to simply "own it"—the stage, the canvas, the blank piece of paper, the marble, the test, the game, the dance floor, the call to action, the arena, the ring, the studio, the mountain, the camera, the building. They didn't let the ANTs that feed the fear of failure or the quest for perfectionism create barriers.

For example, what's the difference between a Picasso painting and any other? Pablo Picasso owned it! He became the best Pablo Picasso he could, with paintings of blue people with noses and eyes in the "wrong" places. Picasso believed in himself. He probably didn't fret about what others would think of his painting or his sculpture. He had confidence in his creative process, so we accept his art and see for its expression of his point view.

"Do you want to be the power in the world? Then be yourself."
– Ralph Waldo Emerson

Think of the movies, the books, the sports teams, the things that inspire you, your heroes and heroines—what attracts you to these specific expressions is a sense of what wholeness, wholeheartedness, boldness, authenticity, and ownership *look like to you*. Whatever you do, if you do it with your whole heart and all the courage you can muster, you will see failure only as an opportunity for growth—and you will find success.

REST STOP

REMEMBERING
Key words and phrases: Can you define them?

Failure _____

_____

Attachment vs. Commitment _____

_____

Perfectionism _____

_____

A Dedicated Heart _____

_____

Living a Life "On Purpose" _____

_____

REFLECTING
Take time to ponder the following.

What ANTs do you think get in the way of embracing, expressing, and experimenting with your creativity?

_____

_____

_____

_____

_____

_____

_____

How might negatively predicting the future (jumping to conclusions) and disqualifying the positive make you abandon a
dream?

_____

_____

_____

Do you struggle with perfectionism? How might you combat the
ANTs involved?

_____

_____

_____

What does it mean to you to have a "dedicated heart"?

_____

_____

_____

REINFORCING
Try these exercises to reinforce what you've learned.

1) Do you recall a time you gave up on a creative endeavor
because you had a fear of failing? What happened? How might
you have thought your way out of the fear of failing? What balanced thoughts might you have mustered?

_____

_____

_____

_____

2) Make a list of the books, people, art, teams, etc., that inspire you. Once you have your list, try to figure out what, if anything, these have in common. What do the themes running through your list say about who you are?

_____

_____

_____

_____

_____

3) Make a list of some of your "failures." After reading this chapter, figure out which ones were failures only because you labeled them as such. Why did you label the events as failures when they happened? Would you label them that way now?

_____

_____

_____

_____

_____

_____

_____

RECORDING AND RESOLVING

Journal writing is a great tool for learning how to control your thoughts and feelings.

List messages about failure you have heard at home, in school, or in the media that affect you. Label each message with the ANTs involved. Then, beside each ANT, write a positive, balanced thought that could eliminate that ANT as well as empower you to become the best you can be, to cultivate in you a dedicated heart.

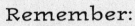

Remember:

EVENTS → INTERPRETATIONS → FEELINGS → ACTIONS

CHANGING FOR GOOD

When you think of the title of this book, *It's Your Mind: Own It!* do you understand what it means? If not, close the book and head back to Page One! Seriously, your *interpretation* of the world has a gigantic influence on your entire life. Taking charge of your mind offers immediate relief from the thoughts that can cause a negative outlook and mood. Taking charge of your mind also has long-term effects on the choices you make and, ultimately, on your destiny. Unfortunately, however, many people don't know this and so they don't think about their own minds nor examine their own thoughts.

If you have not yet put into practice the concepts and ideas in this book, we hope you will start now. If you have been practicing labeling your ANTs and rewriting your stories with realistic, balanced thoughts, we invite you to take a quick inventory of the changes in communication, relationships, and attitudes that have started to occur in your life. If you think these changes are coincidence, think again. Many religions

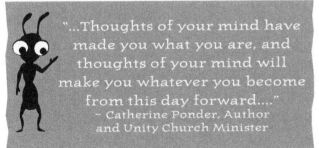

"...Thoughts of your mind have made you what you are, and thoughts of your mind will make you whatever you become from this day forward...."
– Catherine Ponder, Author and Unity Church Minister

and philosophies teach that there is no such thing as a coincidence. Also, as author Agatha Christie's famous detective Miss Marple once said to herself, "Any coincidence is always worth noting. You can throw it away later if it is only a coincidence." In any case, if your life seems to be headed in a better direction, we want you to know where you made the turn.

THE CHALLENGE OF PERMANENT CHANGE

Granted, we know that taking charge of your life and driving its changes takes hard work and doesn't come quickly; people usually change in small steps, one new road at a time. Most importantly, you can't move from the **status quo** (the way things currently are) into new behaviors without going through chaos. Interestingly, motivational speakers often allude to the word *crisis* being illustrated in the Chinese language as a combination of the characters for both *danger* and *opportunity*. Similarly, the nature of the process of change is both vulnerable and tentative.

That is, change can be an opportunity to improve, but it also can be scary territory.

Most of us, in fact, have mixed emotions about the upheaval that change can bring. The biggest emotional hazard may be the nagging voice of the tricky inner critic

who works to keep you in the status quo. That inner critic, threatened by the new possibilities change may bring, can trigger the release of pesky ANTs. Those ANTs might cause you to wonder if those you feel close to won't like the "new you" (jumping to conclusions). When you make the first steps toward a change and slide back to your old ways, the ANTs of all-or-nothing thinking and overgeneralization (about your failed attempts) might chime in. Additional "staying stuck" ANTs might overwhelm you with thoughts such as: "I just didn't want to," "I couldn't help myself," or "It didn't feel good, so I stopped."

Most likely, many Olympic athletes at some point in their training thought these same types of thoughts. But how many top-tier athletes indulged in continuing defeatist thinking? None. They moved past their discomfort to make a change, which led to their eventual greatness.

In general, those who don't get stuck when the road of life gets steep are the ones who grow wise, invent new things, help others, and improve the world. You get the idea! For example, many wise grandparents share stories of past traumas that brought them, along with a great deal of heartache, some of the most important lessons and experiences of their lives. The bottom line is: You can't control what you're handed in this life, but you can control how you interpret your experiences and use them as an opportunity to learn and grow.

As we have been saying throughout this manual, your perception shapes your attitude, which then shapes your feelings. And your feelings, in turn, impact all that you do and don't do. Have you ever heard the old adage, "Whether you think you can or you can't, you're right"? This little sound bite says a lot about the power of what you tell yourself. Once you commit to any self-talk, you will unconsciously go about making your prophecy come true—whether that self-talk contains thinking errors or balanced, realistic thoughts.

THE STAGES OF CHANGE

The Greek philosopher Heraclitus, who lived 2500 years ago, said, "The only thing that is constant is change." In other words, despite anything and everything, the process of change in your life *will* occur. The big question is: Who will be sitting at the steering wheel as you navigate through your life?

Throughout this workbook, we have been challenging *you* to take control. It's your life; own it! We also have been trying to prepare you for some of the predictable curves that lie ahead on the road of life. When you know the road hazards and expect detours, you'll be able to navigate your life by keeping your eyes on the horizon. Also, being able to keep a positive, upbeat attitude along the way might be helped through an understanding of the predictable stages of change. These stages of change— originally outlined by Martin Broadwell, a guru in the field of management—are applicable to acquiring any new skill, but we will look at how they apply to learning to change your own mind.

In general, our mission has been to teach you a new skill, that of observing what you are thinking, monitoring your thoughts for ANTs, and replacing your negative thoughts with balanced or positive ones. As you master the skill of exterminating your ANTs—and make the process a permanent part of your viewpoint—you will go through the following stages of change that will result in a permanent change in your thinking style.

Stage 1: Unconscious Incompetence

In this stage, you don't even realize you need to make a change. You don't know you aren't good at something, so you

don't see the benefit of a change. It's like a baby who doesn't know she can't ride a bike, because she doesn't even know there is such a thing. Putting this stage in perspective of this book, perhaps you haven't yet felt the usefulness of ANT control, so you don't see the benefits of what you're reading about the destructive power of ANTs.

Stage 2: Conscious Incompetence

During this stage, you recognize something you're doing is creating discomfort or that something is less than optimal in your situation. You may recognize you are thinking, feeling, and acting in a way that is harmful to your friends, your family, your school work, or your-self. You're aware of your behavior and know there must be a better way, but you don't know or forgot how to do things differently. What makes this stage painful is that, although you now see there is a prob-lem, you don't know how to change it. But this also is the stage that's filled with "light-bulb" moments.

At this stage you really have to watch your inner critic's tendency toward "should" statements. During this stage, the "Mother of All Criticism" can needle you with many reasons you aren't doing something right as well as with many reasons something isn't safe to try. But, if you curb negative self-talk, this can be an exciting stage! In order to have the motivation to work to acquire a new skill, you have to realize that you lack a desired skill and that having the skill would help you.

Stage 3: Conscious Competence

During Stage 3, you are able to do the skill, but you still have to think about the skill as you do it. For example, right now you have com-pleted this "driver's manual" and have a good grasp on catching your mood becoming negative; you can sit down and think through the ANTs that are affecting your mood. You know that something is off in your thinking, and you know what to do to stop the downward spiral. You also know you have choice; you can choose to engage in destruc-tive behavior and act on a thinking error—or not. Now, however, you also have the ability to revisit the behavior or thinking, analyze your choice, and resolve to make a different choice the next time you encounter a similar experience.

Stage 4: Unconscious Competence

By this stage, you've become so good at the skill of replacing negative thoughts that the process is hard wired into your brain. Granted, you may notice a few uninvited ANTs scouring the few mind crumbs left, but mostly you will just stay out of thinking errors and non-productive behaviors. Analyzing your ANTs and replacing them with realistic, balanced thoughts is now automatic, just a part of you. In a given situation, you may notice something is going wrong, and you will use skilled behavior or challenge your thinking errors. Note: You can only get to this stage by years of practice, practice, practice!

RECAP OF THE STAGES OF CHANGE

1. **Unconscious Incompetence:** You walk away from a rough situation feeling uncomfortable or miserable with no idea what just happened. You probably blame, personalize, label yourself, jump to conclusions, and every other ANT.

2. **Conscious Incompetence:** In a tough situation, you notice what you're thinking but don't know or recall how to change it in the moment. You might think, "Boy, I could have dealt with that differently, but how?" You feel motivated to figure it out.

3. **Conscious Competence:** In the same situation, you still have ANTs crop up regularly, but you now know the skill to change your mood or state of mind. You are able to take deliberate action toward ANT control.

4. **Unconscious Competence:** You now automatically think in a more positive manner without even noticing you're doing it. The less infrequent times you do notice ANTs or negative behavior, you analyze and adjust immediately. You notice what you're doing and change your behavior or reaction. The change is hard wired.

WHY BOTHER? EMBRACING THE CHALLENGE

Why should you do all the hard work it takes to change from an unconscious, reactive person who is sometimes troubled with thinking errors? Why take up the challenge at all? We authors happen to think that deep down inside, or right there on the surface, you want to be the whole person you were born to be. As a young person, you are the future of the world. You know that shaping a healthier future for us all requires the healthiest version of you.

All the major positive shapers of our world overcame the obstacles of negative thinking. Don't think they weren't free of negative thinking! They overcame their obstacles and bequeathed us art, music, governments, literature, spiritual perspectives, scientific discoveries, and new technology. Truly, how you think today will determine not only how happy you are right now, but it also will contribute to every choice you make from this day forward. Your thoughts will make you brave or keep you small. Your thoughts will bring you love and connection or they will contribute to your isolation. Your thoughts will help you to be resilient and rise above adverse situations, or your thoughts will cause you to perpetuate the ugly cycle of mistreatment.

Our philosopher friend Heraclitus captured the essence of our message so well when he wrote, "The soul is dyed the color of its thoughts. Think only on those things that are in line with your principles and can bear the light of day. The content of your character is your choice. Day by day, what you do is who you become. Your integrity is your destiny. It is the light that guides your way."

One person who exemplifies not letting ANTs deter her from the being the best she could be is Helen Keller. There are probably few individuals in our society who have not heard of her. Although born with normal health, by 19-months-old Helen was blind, mute, and deaf. Her thoughts

"You're a person a lot longer before and after you're a professional athlete.
People always say to me, 'Your image is this, your image is that.' Your image isn't your character. Character is what you are as a person. That's what I worry about."
– Derek Jeter,
New York Yankees Baseball Player

as a young girl were filled with hopelessness, and she couldn't even express those thoughts because she was trapped in her own mind without a means of communication. At first Helen resisted change because it was really hard. For example, she had to stop living with her parents and live only with her teacher, Anne Sullivan. The adversities Helen faced could have stopped her from achieving much of anything. Instead, with the help of her teacher and her family, she rose to the challenge and became a noted author, political activist, and lecturer. Her incredible triumph is a beacon of light, hope, and inspiration to all.

Like Helen, you were not born to believe negative self-talk. You were not born to stay small. You were born to grow into your power, into your full and beautiful self.

THRIVING, NOT JUST SURVIVING

When you build certain practices into your daily life, you will move from simply surviving the difficulties of adolescence to thriving in your quest to live a happy, creative, and purposeful existence. There is truly an art to thriving. Just as some plants will *survive* because they get enough sunlight and nutrients from the soil and other plants will *thrive* with an abundance of flowers and fruit, your life can be like the well-fed, brilliant plant if you add a few extra practices. The practices that will help you to thrive—and also enable you to take control of the steering wheel of your life—are balance, stress management, and gratitude.

> **"It is not our darkness that we are afraid of. It is that we are powerful beyond belief."**
> - Author Marianne Williamson

BALANCE

In simple terms, balance is claiming the full plate of life and ensuring you get proper nutrition from all the food groups! For example, sugar can be yummy, but, as an entire meal, it poses serious health risks. Similarly, if you're an avid skateboarder but you do nothing else, you are probably neglecting other areas of your life that are very important to your well-being. Also, if you tend toward perfectionism, you run a high risk of spending too much of your precious time in one area of your life and not enough all around.

A balanced life allows ample time for rest, play, movement, socializing, reflection, and creativity. Achieving a balanced life requires discipline. Any of us can get swept up in the activities of the moment and forget to eat, sleep, rest, do the tasks that pile up, or just step back and reflect. Balance also means setting boundaries and saying "no."

Some common ANTs that can get in the way of balance include jumping to the conclusion that saying "no" means missing out on something; mind reading that others will judge your decision; and all-or-nothing thoughts such as, "If I chose to stay home, I'll never be invited again."

Each of us has an inner rebel that fights against being controlled—even if we're trying to do something good for ourselves such as finding balance. Our Rx for dealing with your inner rebel is to have a chat. Talk to your inner rebel. Make a deal with your inner rebel that you won't forget his or her needs and desires. Then, create balance in your life a little at a time. You can set goals for a balanced day or week. If you don't reach these goals, watch out for all-or-nothing thinking that will contribute to remaining unbalanced. The Mother of All Criticism can really jump all over you if you set goals and don't follow through. If you remember that you are best motivated by encouraging thoughts, you can challenge yourself to turn the "woulda-shoulda-coulda" thoughts into a plan for action.

MANAGING YOUR STRESS

Everyone has stress in his or her life; stress is unavoidable and inescapable. Some stresses, though, we wouldn't want to escape, because they're caused

by experiences that enrich our lives. Graduation, applying to college, and taking the final exams to pass high school are all stressful events, but they're wonderful, too. It's how we view our stressors that will determine the impact stress has on our lives.

In order to keep stress under control, you need to determine whether a given stressful situation is one in which you should avoid, alter, adapt to, or accept the stressor. Knowing how to respond to a stressor is half the means of managing stress.

Avoiding the stressor usually means you have to say "no"; perhaps avoid people who stress you out; stop sweating the small stuff; take control of your environment by shutting off an upsetting program or studying in a quiet place; and cut down on your to-do list or activities. There are many situations in life where you can avoid stress—if you plan ahead.

Altering the stressor often involves being a better communicator. If you express your feelings and needs versus bottling things up, your stress will be lower. Or, you might need to be more assertive so that people and situations don't bulldoze you. You also might need to be more honest with people about your limitations. For example, if you have a big test tomorrow and your BFF wants to unload her day onto you, you may need

> **"How we tell our stories matters. Stories are held in our brain in shapes. When we change the story, that shape will change."**
> - Jonah Willihnganz,
> Professor at Stanford Univ. & Director of the Stanford Storytelling Project

to let her know you can talk for only 15 minutes. Poor time management also can result in stress, so you need to learn how to plan and not over-extend yourself. If you need help managing time, check out the many books and apps out there or turn to the supportive adults in your life.

Adapting to the stressor requires knowing when the stress is unavoidable and unchangeable, so you have no choice but to change. You can reduce these types of stressful situations by changing your expectations and your attitude—and by upping your ANT control efforts. In other words, avoid thoughts of should, never, always, and must; all these ANTs increase stress by suggesting that the stressor is your fault, or that you are somehow jinxed with bad luck. A traffic jam is a good example of an unavoidable stress. There's nothing you can do in the situation, even if you're going to be late. So you can sit in stalled traffic telling yourself you should have gone a different route or left earlier, or you can take the time to breathe, relax, and listen to a new radio station. That's adapting by shifting your attitude and staying positive. People who ask themselves, "What is it I can learn in this situation?" are practicing this type of stress management.

Accepting a stressor can be difficult, because inside of us is a little kid who still believes that, if we complain or protest enough, the universe will hear and change the situation. We all need to learn to accept unavoidable stressors such as the death of a loved one, rejection from a partner, the divorce of our parents, failing to get into that top choice college, and betrayals of friends. The alcohol recovery program AA captures this option well in its well-known motto that goes like this: "God, grant me the serenity to accept the things I cannot change, the courage to change the things I can, and the wisdom to know the difference." What you can do to reduce the pain of unavoidable stressors is to share your feelings with a trusted person, forgive those who have hurt you, and turn toward practices that bring you inner strength such as prayer.

In essence, you need to learn to live a life that keeps your strength and resilience high. How can you do this? Relax! Relaxation habits can cultivate in you a healthy stress tolerance. Meditation is one such habit that has been viewed by numerous cultures throughout the world as a powerful relaxation and stress management tool. The way meditation works is that you empty your mind of chatter, observe any thoughts, and then "let go" of them without dwelling on whether they are good, bad, right, or wrong. This goes a long way toward keeping negative thoughts under control.

Many of us think of meditation as sitting still and straight with our eyes closed for an extended period of time. While not untrue, this is really just one of the many forms of meditation. You can meditate by creating art, in song, or by contemplating nature or movement. These days, learning to meditate is as easy as watching meditation practices on television, listening to guided audio meditations on your phone, or downloading video tutorials online. If you participate in an organized religion, you might investigate how your particular religion practices meditation or, by another name, contemplation. Other aspects of religion and spirituality are helpful as stress reducers as well. Prayer, spiritual studies, inspirational personal growth, singing in a choir, solitude, spiritual community, and attending worship services are some of the many positive and constructive ways to utilize your spiritual self to manage your stress.

We believe that balancing your thoughts—whether by practicing ANT control or by meditating—is the strongest means by which you can manage stress. But you can blow off steam in many other ways: exercise, create art, get lost in a hobby, spend time in nature, listen to or play music, call a friend, take a hot bath or shower, play a game alone or with others, read, stretch or do yoga, light scented candles, make a collage, drink a cup of tea, write in your journal, watch a funny (not scary) movie, or play with your pet. There are, in fact, as many positive outlets for stress as there are humans.

GRATITUDE

Thanks to the fact that **gratitude** is a much-researched topic in psychology, we know that spending a few minutes per day thinking about the things for which you are grateful has far-reaching rewards. Only a few years ago, people thought gratitude was something completely "religious." Now mental health professionals know that practicing gratitude has essential benefits in curing depression, increasing overall happiness, and improving failing health.

Some counselors suggest you schedule for yourself a two-minute daily gratitude session. You can sit, kneel, lie on your bed, or go for a walk in the neighborhood. During this dedicated time, wherever you are, you write or say aloud the things for which you are grateful. You also can use the session time to write in your journal, share your thoughts with a friend, or pray.

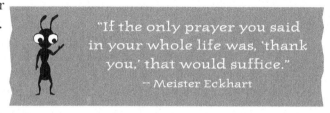

"If the only prayer you said in your whole life was, 'thank you,' that would suffice."
– Meister Eckhart

Gratitude sessions are wonderful opportunities to turn negatives into positives. As you think about the positive benefits of your efforts, you can reframe any ANTs. When you are stretching to see beyond your challenges, you can be grateful that you have challenges. Having challenges implies you are alive and trying to participate proactively in your life. Gratitude sessions, in fact, usually improve your mood within minutes. When you make gratitude sessions a regular practice, you'll also see major improvement in your baseline happiness.

Truly, having an "attitude of gratitude" is the ultimate ANT control. Through the practice, you rewire your brain toward positive thoughts and toward reframing negative events. Ultimately, gratitude helps remind you of what's really important. "I am grateful for the opportunity to go to a good school" is, in the long run, much more valuable to your well-being than, "There is so much homework at this stupid school!" Gratitude also helps you to return a favor and to remember to say, "Thank you," perhaps in the form of a thank-you card or text. In addition, making a gratitude list will help you to remember that you don't have a good life all on your own. Others play a major role as "co-pilots" as you navigate your life!

BE THANKFUL

Be thankful that you don't already have everything you desire,
If you did, what would there be to look forward to?
Be thankful when you don't know something,
For it gives you the opportunity to learn.
Be thankful for the difficult times.
During those times you grow.
Be thankful for your limitations,
Because they give you opportunities for improvement.
Be thankful for each new challenge,
Because it will build your strength and character.
Be thankful for your mistakes.
They will teach you valuable lessons.
Be thankful when you're tired and weary,
Because it means you've made a difference.
It is easy to be thankful for the good things.
A life of rich fulfillment comes to those who are
also thankful for the setbacks.
Gratitude can turn a negative into a positive.
Find a way to be thankful for your troubles
and they can become your blessings.
~ Author Unknown ~

YOU CAN CHANGE YOUR LIFE

We all have a destination (or many destinations) we hope to reach. We are all navigating our own paths on our own journeys. Some of us will want the vehicle of our lives to be a bus packed with friends and colleagues, and some of us will want to drive a mini with just our own thoughts to keep us company.

Whoever you are, whatever your goals, you were born with everything needed to reach your destinations. All you have to do is to understand the engine of your mind. Will it run in tiptop shape and get you there quickly? Or will you run out of gas or into a tree? Will you clunk along? Or will you happily cruise with the windows down and the wind blowing through your hair?

Having read through this manual (and, hopefully, having done some of the "Rest Stop" exercises), you are now armed with the awareness and the tools to not only map your route, but also to stay on the road by avoiding obstacles and dead ends. Who and what and how you are remain always in your keeping. Own your mind, and you *will* change your life.

> "In order that the mind should see light instead of darkness, so the entire soul must be turned away from this changing world, until its eye can learn to contemplate reality and that supreme splendor which we have called the good.
> Hence, there may well be an art whose aim would be to affect this very thing."
> – Philosopher Socrates

REST STOP

REMEMBERING
Key words and phrases: Can you define them?

Status Quo _____

_____

_____

Adapting to Stress _____

_____

_____

Accepting Stress _____

_____

_____

Gratitude _____

_____

_____

REFLECTING
Take time to ponder the following.

How balanced is your life? If you divide your life into parts
(e.g., school, family, health, friendships, finances, recreation,
spirituality, etc.), where do you spend the majority of your time?
Where do you spend the least? Is there anything you want to do
more? Less? Change?

_____

_____

_____

_____

_____

_____

_____

_____

_____

_____

_____

_____

_____

_____

_____

What stressor has troubled you recently? Looking back, did you avoid it, alter it, adapt to it, or accept it? How successful was your strategy? Now that you have read about managing stress, would you like to have responded differently?

_____

_____

_____

_____

_____

_____

_____

_____

REINFORCING

Try this exercise to reinforce what you've learned.

On the following page, we're including a blank mood log to help you become self-actualized in your life. We hope you'll copy it and use it as a tool in the future during any situation when you're confronting ANTs.

MOOD LOG

Event:

What Emotions I Notice:

Negative Thoughts:

Thinking Errors:

Balanced/Replacement Thoughts:

Actions I Can Take:

RECORDING AND RESOLVING

Journal writing is a great tool for learning how to control your thoughts and feelings.

What are your personal beliefs about your ability to change? Write about them and watch out for any ANTs! Label each ANT and replace it with a balanced thought. Have you tried before and failed? Have you tried to make changes and succeeded? What happened?

Think of a new behavior or a skill you have worked on in the past. Write about the stages you remember going through while perfecting the skill.

Challenge yourself to a two-minute gratitude practice for a month. Write what you are grateful for and then read your list aloud to someone.

_____

_____

_____

_____

_____

_____

_____

_____

_____

_____

_____

_____

_____

_____

_____

_____

_____

_____

_____

_____

_____

_____

Remember:

EVENTS → INTERPRETATIONS → FEELINGS → ACTIONS

References

Welcome to Your "Driver's Manual"

p. 2 • Burns, David D. *Feeling Good: The New Mood Therapy*. NY: Harper, 2008.

p. 3 • UCLA Laboratory of Neuro Imaging, 2008.

Your Brain: Your Greatest Asset

p. 11 • Badenoch, Bonnie. *Being a Brain-Wise Therapist: A Practical Guide to Interpersonal Neurobiology*. NY: W. Norton and Co., 2008.

p. 13 • Stokes, Timothy B. *What Freud Didn't Know: A Three-Step Practice for Emotional Well-Being through Neuroscience and Psychology*. Piscataway Township, NJ: Rutgers Univ. Press, 2009.

p. 16 • Burns, David D. *Feeling Good: The New Mood Therapy*. NY: Harper, 2008.

p. 17 • Siegel, Daniel J. *Brainstorm: The Power and Purpose of the Teenage Brain*. NY: Tarcher, 2014.

Coping with Unhelpful Anger

p. 68 • Emmons, Robert A. and Michael E. McCullough. "Counting blessings versus burdens: An experimental investigation of gratitude and subjective well-being in daily life." *Journal of Personality and Social Psychology*, 84 (Feb. 2003): 377-389. doi: 10.1037/0022-3514.84.2.377.

p. 72 • U.S. Department of Education, National Center for Educational Statistics (2013). "Student reports of bullying and cyber-bullying: Results from the 2011 school crime supplement to the national crime victimization survey."

• Center for Disease Control, National Center for Injury Prevention and Control (2012). "Understanding bullying."

• Petrosino, A., S. Guckenburg, J. DeVoe and T. Hanson. Institute of Education Sciences (2010). "What characteristics of bullying, bullying victims, and schools are associated with increased reporting of bullying to school officials?" Washington, DC: National Center for Education Evaluation and Regional Assistance.

• Hawkins, D. L., D. J. Pepler and W. M. Craig. "Naturalistic observations of peer interventions in bullying." *Social Development,* 10, no. 4 (2001): 512-527.

p. 73 • Davis, Stan and C. L. Nixon. *Youth Voice Project: Student Insights into Bullying and Peer Mistreatment.* Champaign, IL: Research Press, 2014.

Managing Anxiety
p. 93 • Family Institute at Northwestern University. "Cyber bullying more difficult for teenagers to process psychologically than in-person bullying." *ScienceDaily*, 6 (Nov. 2013).

Dealing with Depression
p. 101 • National Institute of Mental Health Factsheet (2014). http://www.nimh.nih.gov/health/publications/depression-in-children-and-adolescents/index.shtml. Accessed July 31, 2014.

p. 102 • Masarie, K., K. Keller Jones, R. Matinko-Wald, J. Bellant Scheer, C. Dickson and M. Terner. *Face to Face: Cultivating Kids' Social Lives in Today's Digital World.* Portland, OR: Family Empowerment Network, 2014.

Understanding Relationships

p. 126 • Gottman, John M. and Nan Silver. *The Seven Principles for Making Marriage Work: A Practical Guide from the Country's Foremost Relationship Expert.* NY: Harmony Books, 2000.

• Hendrix, Harville. *Getting the Love You Want: A Guide for Couples.* NY: Holt and Co., Rev. 2007.

Practicing Compassion

p. 143 • Quote reprinted by permission from Ruth Fishel. From her *The Journey Within: A Spiritual Path to Recovery.* Deerfield Beach, FL: HCI Books, 1987.

Getting Motivated

p. 161 • Eker, T. Harv. *Secrets of the Millionaire Mind: Mastering the Inner Game of Wealth.* NY: HarperBusiness, 2005.

Finding the Success in Failure

p. 175 • Haatai, Bob. "6 Leadership Lessons from Pete Carroll." (Feb. 4, 2014). http://bobhaa.com/6-things-learned-pete-carroll-leadership. Accessed August 2, 2014.

Changing for Good

p. 183 • Broadwell, Martin M. and C. Broadwell Dietrich. *"The New Supervisor: How to Thrive in Your First Year As a Manager."* NY: Basic Books, 1998.

Meet the Authors

Nicole Jon Sievers, MSW, LCSW, is dedicated to advocacy and passionate about promoting social justice. For over 25 years, she has worked with youth and the systems serving them. She is celebrated for inspiring adolescents to summon courage, humility, and resilience. Her diverse roles have included counselor, certified Imago relationship therapist, school teacher, educational district consultant, Outward Bound instructor, and forensic consultant.

Nicole drives initiatives. She has brought Nobel Peace Prize Laureates to schools for collaborative problem solving, she has raised funds for peace concerts, she has hosted dinners at her home for humanitarian figures including a U.S. presidential candidate, and she even once shared a dance with Mick Jagger onstage!

Recognizing that peer-to-peer incentives are an unusually potent means of diminishing bullying behavior, Nicole founded the Stand for Courage Foundation (www.standforcourage.org) in 2011. In 2014, the American Psychological Association honored the Foundation with a Visionary Award that will support further research of program efficacy.

As a result of her extensive training, diverse experience, and unique vision, Nicole has consulted, taught, and been a guest speaker on the public stage; her radio and television guest appearances have been aired locally, nationally, and internationally. Nicole also has contributed to many publications including books, magazines, and newspapers. *It's Your Mind: Own It!* is her first book.

In addition, Nicole is frequently invited to participate in various organizations. One role of which she is particularly excited is as a Seattle Music Commissioner (www.cityofmusic.com/music-commission). As a member of the Music Commission, she joins a diverse group of community, business, and industry leaders who guide Seattle's efforts to support, promote, expand, and encourage Seattle's vibrant music culture.

Nicole, her husband Eric, and their five sons live in Seattle.

Norene Gonsiewski, MSW, LCSW, has worked with couples and individuals since 1980 using Cognitive Behavioral Therapy. Dedicated to helping people of all ages to understand how our thinking determines our lives, Norene has coached thousands of people not only to improve their moods and manage depression and anxiety but also to improve their marriages, work relationships, and family lives. Together with Nicole, she has taught many workshops and classes for teenagers and their parents in the areas of ANTs and communication.

In 1997, Norene founded Portland Relationship Center, through which she practices Imago Relationship Therapy and offers resources for creating healthy and lasting relationships. She teaches workshops for couples and individuals on how to building lasting and passionate relationships. She also teaches Money Habitudes™, a course for adults and teens on understanding your habits and attitudes about money. These offerings and more can be found at her website: www.portlandrelationshipcenter.com.

Norene is affectionately known at the "Relationship Guru." As such, she is a sought-after guest on television talk shows. She loves working with parents on the challenges that arise inside themselves and in their marriage while raising a family. In today's world, those challenges can last even longer as young adult children continue to live at home.

In addition to co-authoring *It's Your Mind: Own It!* Norene also is the co-author of *Rock Solid Relationship: How to Build a Safe and Passionate Relationship* as well as *A Training Manual for Respite*, a book focusing on the importance of respite care for families with children with medical needs.

Norene lives in Portland, Oregon, with her husband, Tom.